SEVENTEENTH CENTURY
SONGS AND LYRICS

SEVENTEENTH CENTURY
SONGS AND LYRICS

Collected and edited from the
original music manuscripts

By

John P. Cutts

Granger Index Reprint Series

BOOKS FOR LIBRARIES PRESS
FREEPORT, NEW YORK

STANDARD BOOK NUMBER:
8369-6055-6

LIBRARY OF CONGRESS CATALOG CARD NUMBER:
70-80373

MANUFACTURED
BY
HALLMARK LITHOGRAPHERS, INC.
IN THE U.S.A.

CONTENTS

INTRODUCTION

THIS BOOK is intended as a continuation of the late Norman Ault's work. It was he who began to explore music MSS for unknown lyrics several of which he published in his anthologies, *Elizabethan Lyrics,* 1928, *A Treasury of Unfamiliar Lyrics,* 1938 and *Seventeenth Century Lyrics,* 1928 revised 1950. Ault sampled the few MSS he consulted since they were for the most part uncatalogued and had not been examined and described in detail. I have been at work cataloguing each entry in the MSS and checking with all the printed sources I could personally consult. The result is that over 400 lyrics and songs are unidentifiable and are, I presume, unknown. It is these which I now wish to present before the reader.

Of course, there will always be the possibility that some of these lyrics may prove after all to be reasonably well known. When such a great authority as Ault himself printed George Herbert's "Peace muttring thoughts" as unknown from an MS source there is all the greater possibility that one with only a few years' experience might commit similar errors. A few of the lyrics given here were indeed printed in the Seventeenth Century in collections which are now so rare that they are almost as inaccessible as the manuscripts, hence my decision to include them. I beg my readers' indulgence and ask that any identification of the material now presented be made known to me so that future anthologies may benefit from the joint attention of those interested in Seventeenth Century songs and lyrics.

Seventeenth-century music MSS have been widely scattered since their origination and it is only by the use of microfilm that I have been able to reassemble them. Wherever possible I have personally consulted the MSS in addition to procuring complete microfilms.

The relationship between poet and musician in the Seventeenth Century has never been fully explored because there has hitherto been a dearth of evidence. It will be some time before anyone is in a position to collate all the actual music,* but the results so far are encouraging. It has long been known that Henry Lawes composed music specially for Milton, but what is not realized is that Henry Lawes almost had a monopoly with Thomas Carew's poetry, as his

---

*The present writer has this work in progress.

brother William had with John Suckling's, John Gamble with Thomas Stanley's (until he was superseded by John Wilson) and John Wilson with Richard Lovelace's. Herrick's poetry seems to have attracted both Henry and William Lawes. Nicholas Lanier, Alfonso Ferrabosco, Robert Johnson and William Lawes set Ben Jonson's poetry to music.

Some of the MSS contain distinct groups of songs by particular poets and in the midst of these there are occasional ones that have never been ascribed to the poets. Thus it would seem possible to offer a suggestion of authorship from the position which a poem occupies in a certain manuscript collection. The near proximity of recognizable poems may suggest, too, the same author. The final criterion must be that of style, however, and it is for this reason that it is especially important that readers should have the original texts before them to form their own opinions.

I have already described several of the MSS in article form in magazines and have printed certain unidentified lyrics with requests to readers for identification. Hitherto, not a single poem I have printed as anonymous has been pointed out to me as already having been printed, though I myself have been able to ascertain that one or two have indeed been so under slightly different first lines.

This fact suggests the necessity of a note to the effect that for some reason certain printed lyrics preserved quite a different stanza order in MSS and occasionally the very first printed stanza is displaced with the result that a first line index fails to identify it.

There is no consistency within the separate MSS themselves with regard to the use of capitalizations, contractions and spelling. Nor would there seem to be any consistency in the indication of the metrical and stanzaic form of the poem when verses, other than those that are actually laid under the musical notation, are given separately at the side or foot of the music. The extra verses, however, usually given a numerical order, often help to determine exactly what repetitions in the underlaid text are due to the musician's license. When there is *only* the underlaid text it is sometimes difficult to distinguish between musician's license and genuine repetition. Moreover, in these cases it is often impossible to know whether or no the text is intended to be divided into stanzas. If the music simply repeats itself for divisions these become clear, but when the poem is "throughset" like a continuous composition then one can no longer be certain of the division into verses, and in such cases I have felt no justification for dividing the text.

I have scrupulously maintained the readings of the MSS and have suggested emendation in brackets. The Notes will explain any MS peculiarity and any emendation.

How to arrange the songs presented a very real difficulty. Ault's attempt to arrange by chronology was reasonably assured since he worked principally from first printed sources and had specific dates to rely on. The music MSS, with very few exceptions, had no specific dating, and I have learnt from eight years' familiarity with them that not very much dependence is to be placed on statements by the library authorities under whose aegis the MSS reside and by whose direction the MSS were tentatively dated for cataloguing purposes. The dating of these MSS depends on a vast amount of research into music MSS of the period—the task of a lifetime.

Arrangement of the songs in this collection, therefore, could not be chronological. It seemed at first that an arrangement by subject might suit our present purposes but it soon became evident that a subject index would have to be broken down into so many divisions, there being so much overlapping within even a single lyric, that its usefulness would be seriously impaired. The poets themselves in their collections did not seem to follow, for the most part, any specific arrangement in presenting their poems though each poem was given a title of some kind.

After a great deal of thought I decided to present the lyrics in strict alphabetical order by first lines and to provide a fairly comprehensive subject index at the back of the book to act as a guide.

I wish to make a general acknowledgment to all the library authorities by whose permission I have been allowed to procure microfilms of and to print unpublished material from the various music MSS in their keeping. Personal acknowledgment is due to Professor Allardyce Nicoll, Head of the Shakespeare Institute, Stratford-Upon Avon, who first fostered in me the idea to build up a microfilm collection of seventeenth-century music MSS; to Mr. J. M. Nosworthy, Lecturer in the English Department of the University of South Wales, Aberystwyth, for his continual encouragement; to Dean Henry Bent, Professor Hardin Craig, and Professor William Peden of the University of Missouri, whose understanding and stimulation made it possible for me to complete this book during my year as a Visiting Assistant Professor at the University of Missouri.

JOHN P. CUTTS

Harke this lesson
Serue God euer
Credit not all y^t thow Hearest
Say not all y^t thow Thinkest
Desire not all y^t thow Seest
Spend not all y^t thow Hast
Doe not all y^t thow Maist
But of all thinges take heed of the Beginninge
See the Middle and praise the endinge
Doo that wch is good say that is true
Cherish old frende chaung for no new.

A boat a boat haste to the ferry

A boat a boat haste to the ferry,
for wee'l go over to be merry
to laugh and sing, and drink old sherry.

Squyer MS.490.76.

A fastinge Supper call you this

A fastinge Supper call you this
          O pallats blisse,
two gentle puddinges Soft & white,
          fill'd with delight.
Such as noe Muse could Euer maKe,
          for Poets SaKe,
Such as Loue fedd on when ye Boy,
          was nurst by Troy.
Since when like to his Bow they stand
          fixt to his hand.
food fitt for Ladyes who yet finde,
          In all the Kinde
of puddinges none such pleasure giues
          as that wch liues.

Edinburgh University Library MS.Dc.1.69.163.

A vsless pipe stop I haue been

A vsless pipe stop I haue been
A viol broken & uns[t]rung,
as dayly frightments I had seen
vnto my roofe still claue my tonge
Then whisperd I to him that lent
mee breath at first & breath hee sent
vnto his fainting Instrument

To him the first fruites of my voyce
Ile pay in thankefull melody
my hart shall wth my lungs reioyce
& on my breath my soule shall fly
If [h]is people after mee shall sing
his spirrits words to mine shall bring
wherwth Ile make his Temple ring,

when vnto Fals or Idle words
frome truth or from sobriety
my lips decline or send out swords
to wound my neighbour secretly.
O then I wish I may obtaine
my olde disease mee to restraine
And to speake well new speech againe.

B.M.Add.MS.29396,ff.83ᵛ,84.

About with this brimmer my bullyes

About with this brimmer my bullyes
to each Royallist turn'd out of line
theire gibbitts & strapado pullies
vnited hearts shall not disioyne
this stratagines meant to an honest intent
for out of our enimies care
this Proiects contriued to make us long liu'd
by shuning infectious ayre
ther london smoke like to a poys'nous dart
will presently strike to a treu loyall heart.

A second cup I must importune
Ile haue itt to run round the table
to all the stout souldiers of fortune
that will drinke and say when theire able
to want & to owe is an honour wee know
and easily may be attested
if monyes come short ittl passe not the courte
for a prine [prince?] may himselfe be acosted
Hee needes must aduenture such men to adore
that will not lets enter to looke one our score

Here freely wee may with eache other
carouse and discourse of our marches
of this enterprize and the tother
& pish att theire tapes & searches
The maior of the citty we heartily pitty
and wisht him in our condition
then no Jealous head coo'd hã rais'd him frõ bed
to make him a stocke of derision
A third cup about to his maiestyes freinds
weele drinke itt all out though our bladders itt rends.

Drexel MS.4041,ff.112ᵛ,113.

5

Adieu? why so? deare Castaminda stay

Charus   : Adieu? why so? deare Castaminda stay
Castaminda : for wt? Charus be quick else Ile away
Charus   : That's a heart-deading-sound *Cast* : This is dissem-
                    bling
Charus   : Deaths shaking horror cañot cause more trembling
Castaminda : Leave these ill governd passions of wt ailes yee?
Charus   : I faint alas because my Love she failes me
Castaminda : Wt is she? Beauty shines to yeild reflection
Charus   : A gracefull modell of unstain'd perfection
Castaminda : How yn? *Charus* : Thats all I know for to this hower
                    I smothred stiffling flames & had no power
                    To beg all cooling moisture a bedewed kisse
Castaminda : Such barren gamesters nere attaine to blisse
Charus   : This is my fault & since I make confession
                    Let me seale up those lipps wth this impression
Castaminda : They can no more accuse thee whilst yt thus
                    Or joint affections signe ymselves to us.

Bod.Lib.MS.Don.c.57,ff.62ᵛ-63.

6

Admit thou darlinge of myne Eyes

Admit thou darlinge of myne Eyes,
A haue some Idols lately framde,
yt vnderneath a falce disguise,
our true loue might ye less be famde,
canst thou yt knowst my hart,
Suppose I fall from thee, to worship those?

Remember deere, how loath & slow,
I was to cast a looke or smyle,
or one loue-lyne to misbestow
till thou hadst changd both face & stile,
And art thou growne affraide to see
yt Maske put on thou madst for me.

I dare not call those childish feares
wch com from loue, much less from thee
but wash awaye wth frequent teares
this Counterfeit Idolatrye
And Hencforth kneele at Nev'ra shrine
to blinde ye world but onely thyne.

B.M.Loan MS.35,f.58ᵛ.

Ah, ah ye falce fatall tale I read

Ah, ah ye falce fatall tale I read,
when my hart Heedless and vnwise
first studied & falce Coṁented,
on th' vnknowne texte of thy lou'de Eyes;
when thy glibe runinge lauish tongue,
showred downe more Oathes thy faith t'avow,
then Morninge dewes on flowers are Hunge
or blossoms on ye Suṁer bough;
soe was my sillye truth betraide,
by a smooth tongue and wininge Eye,
poisons by wch theres many'a Mayde,
has perishd sure as well as I.

Ah loue! where is thy Abydinge?

Ah loue! where is thy Abydinge?
or in my hart, or in her Eyes resydinge:
if I admyre thy splendor,
in her fayre Eyes thou shinest;
if now [how?] thou woundst & burnst my hart to Cinder,
thou in my hart remaynest:
O if to show thy wonders,
thou beest willinge,
or powre in wretches killinge,
Change thy conceipt & Center;
and in myne Eyes, or in her hard Hart Enter.

B.M.Loan 35,f.3ᵛ.

All yee forsaken louers come & pitty my distress

All yee forsaken louers come & pitty my distress
you shall know why, all yee beloued can pitty mee noe less,
for loue I dye, yet hope at last to moue pitty in her brest,
my poore hart, may find some rest,
wch hath so long bene pained,
to shew my distress my faith and my loue vnfayned.

Fitzwilliam MS.52.D,f.111^v.

Amarillis teare thy haire

Amarillis teare thy haire
beat thy breast sigh weepe despaire
Cry Ah me is Daphnis dead?
I see a palenesse in his brow
& his cheekes are drown'd in snow
whither are those roses fled?
o my heart how cold hee's growne!
sure his lips are turnd to stone,
more soft y^n downe his kisses were
Daphnis speake speake speake one gentle word
on our eys one looke afford
canst y^u sleepe when I am here.

Amintor oh thou faithless swane

Amintor oh thou faithless swane,
thus to requite me with disdaine
to Cheate a poor shepherd[e]ss into beleefe
& leauing mee big with dishonour & Greife

I must confess I was betraid
By all ye solemn vows y^u made
yet doe not insult for it may be y^r turne
to meet with disdaine when you really burne.

To scorne mee & laugh at my paine
to Loue me a while and scorne mee againe
If this be if this be the fate you'l alowe
your punishments Just, for breaking your vow.

B.M.Add.MS.29396,f.60.

And why so coy? what is yor Rose

And why so coy? what is yor Rose
if growing better then ye Grasse,
plucke it and smell
and then yor nose will tell
you what a savour 't has,
consider this and I suppose
you'll give me leave to plucke a Rose

The plan'ts when alone we see
Alas how poore their inflvence
Let them in coniunction bee
And then our Masters they commence
Let this be alwayes in thy mind
Thy aspect then wilbe more kind.

Our Mother Earth indures ye plowe
And patiently to give thee Bread
For thou wovldst starve and others too
shovld she keepe hir Maidenhead
Thinke so and then thy froward will
I hope will give me leave to till.

Bod.Lib.MS.Mus.b.1,f.117^v.

Apollo once a yeare may merry be

Apollo once a yeare may merry be,
as many say, but few the reason know,
yet reason knowes, the ofter merry he,
the more our mirth, the lesse ye more our woe
But now in this fayre time, and you and we
men that soe say, may see why they say soe,
for should the sun reioyce but once a yeare,
when should it be but now and why not heere.

ffor if the sun did fame or honour neede
What time like this could fame or honour lend
yf feare he wanted wherein could he speede
Like this that art nor nature cannot mend
yf light he lack's (which heere doth soe exceed)
What beauty like your eyes could him befreind
Then yf the suñ should sing but once a yeere
When should he sing but now & where but heere.

Ch. Ch. MS.Mus.87,ff.17ᵛ,18.

Arise arise, faire Sun restore ye daye

Arise arise, faire Sun restore ye daye,
to ye darkned world, & mee,
frō those Iv'ry gates display,
ye long wish't for Morne, for see,
night & I doe Joyntly weepe,
whilst thyne Eyes are lock't in sleepe,

See ye blushinge East discryes
y^t the Jealous suñ is neere,
& wth double speed him hyes
vnto our vpper Hemisphaere
fearinge least wee Mortalls may,
from thine Eyes mistake ye daye.

Those faint fires y^t rule ye Night,
languish, & ye Am'rous Moone
loosing too her borow'd light
hasts to her Endymion,
only I of all vnblest
wander, void of light & rest.

B.M.Add.MS.11608,ff.34ᵛ,35.

Art thou gon in haste Ile not forsake thee

S : Art thou gon in haste Ile not forsake thee;
      Runst thou nere so fast, Ile ore take thee;
      O're ye dales ore ye downes, through ye dimme shaddowes
      to ye feilds to ye townes, through ye green meddowes

      All along ye playnes to ye highe mountaines,
      vp and downe againe to the low fountaines,
      Eccho then, shall agen, tell thee I follow
      And ye floods, to the woods, carry my hollow.

N : Runst thou ne're so swift, thou shalt not catch me
      but Ile fynde a shift, to Ore match thee
      from thyne Eye will I fly, fast as a swallow
      leauing Ayre, only there, mocking thy hollow.

      Thus from place to place if thou persue me,
      shalt thou run a race but ne're veiw me
      I will run like ye Nun chas'd by Appollo
      Or my weeds into reeds turn if thou follow.

B.M.Loan MS.35,f.183. "A Swaine persuing a Nimphe that flyes him".

Art thou in Loue? it cañot be?

Art thou in Loue? it cañot be?
'twill proue too Great a Raritye!
for loue is Bañishde from ye Mynde,
& Eurye Creature proues vnkinde.

yor Sex wee know hath too much Powre
to be Confinde aboue an Howre
And Ladyes are becom soe wyse
theyle please theyre Owne not Others Eyes

Noe Archers from Aboue are Sent
poore Cupids Bow lyes now vnbent
and weomen Boast that they can fynde
a neerer waye to ease the Mynde

yet still you sighe & keep adoe
only to tempt poor men to wooe
but sure if thou a Louer bee
'tis of thy selfe & not of mee.

B.M.Loan MS.35,f.168.

17

art thou that shee

art thou that shee
then whome noe fayrer is
art thou that shee
desier soe striues to kisse,
say I am how then
maids may not kisse
such wanton humord men.

Art thou that shee
the world commends for witt
art thou soe wise
and makst noe vse of it
Say I am how then
my witt doth teach me shun
such foolish foolish men.

Ch.Ch.MS.439,f.18ᵛ.

As oft I doe record

As oft I doe record
ye pleasures I haue had,
at yonder slide-thrift board
wth many a liuely ladd,
it makes mee merry & gladd,
though it putts mee to micKle paine
Ise would I had seld mine eld white Nagg,
gin Jinny were here againe.

she baK'd & brew'd to sell
To those that passed by
Gead fellowes lou'd her well
Gead feath & sea did I;
for Oh! when I was dry,
Her liquor I might haue tane
Ise wou'd I had tread my shune awry
Gin Jinny were here againe.

A man might for his mony
Haue had twea potts of Ale
Or tasted of a Cony
the head or eKe ye Tayle.
You neuer need to fayle
soe shee were in ye vaine
Alas Alas all flesh is frayle
Wou'd Jinny were here againe.

full oft haue she & I,
All in ye buttery play'd
At tray trip with a dy
And sent away the mayd
She was o' ye dealinge trade
She'd gea yea twea for eane
And yet she was no fulsome Jade
Would Jinny were here againe.

I lig'd mee downe for wea,
And I wept mine eyne out cleene
I'se wou'd poore JocKeyes eyne
My Jinny had neuer seene,
for O : as I doe weene,
She was my beautyes Queene
Ise wou'd that I, poore JocKey might dy
Gin Jinny were here agen.

B.M.Add.MS.29396,ff.16ᵛ,17.

this cash
s all mad
t are they that no mony had:

at's full proues the owner A gull
o great nor aptter to cheate
lanke makes the owner franke
freind his loues wth out end
can bee too frollik and free
ate then a needy mans fate

is cash
all mad
are they that no mony had:

s a stranger then mans out of danger
& from wine hees kept within line
barrels nor broaches no quarrels
f mockes & as many knockes
elfe by scorning of pelfe
no shooes in hunting for newes.

s cash
ll mad
re they that no mony had:

o heires nor shoulden men feares
o rent forgets what was lent
what this toy cost or that
iles nor maketh no wiles
now he treads downe ye world
sumes hee counts vm but scvmes.

cash
mad
they that no mony had:

94ᵛ,95.

24

As on a daye Clorinda fayre was bathinge

As on a daye Clorinda fayre was bathinge
vnto ye silver streames her Selfe bequeathinge;
she syghed thus, Alas poore soule she said;
I feare that I shall dye, shall dye a mayde.

The sheperd Doron, her Enamourd swaine
that longe had lou'de but Euer lou'de in vaine,
douth heer & see, yet durst not see nor heer
such was th' impression of his maiden feare.

Till at the last, Admyringe beautyes wonder
his bashfulnes more powrfull thoughts came vnder
And then he vow'de, wth sighes, wth Oathes, & teares,
that he would dye or Ease Clorinda's feares.

W^th in his Armes, her snow whyte Armes he takes
she streiuinge yeelds, yet willingly mistakes
And wth noe noe, fye fye begon, she swears
sheel run, sheele call, sheele crye, she faineth tears.

When Phillomell the prick felt at her brest
she Easde her sighes, & gaue her passion rest,
And wth sweet sweet, & turninge vp her Eyes
she pants, she sighes, she yeelds, she faints & dyes.

B.M.Loan MS.35,f.6.ᵛ.

21

As tuned harp-strings sad Noates take

As tuned harp-strings sad Noates take,
soe my devided sighes doe shake
thus covld I sigh out breath & life,
would she for pitty fetch a sigh,

As trickling teares from eyes depart
so bleeding dropps fall from my Hart,
Harts bloudy dropps requited were
would she for pitty dropp a teare,

fly God of love to that faire Brest,
and in my name cry there for rest,
yf she refuse, then once more cry,
Alas for pitty & so dye.

Ave rosa sine spiñis

Ave rosa sine spiñis
tu quam pater in divinis
Maiestate sublimavit
et ab omni vi purgavit

Chorus   Salve lux fulgens ut /
supra Lillium pulchr
Corde tuo Summa pi
Clemens dulcis ô Ma
fac nos pia comemorari
. . (.) am mortis tui cha
O pia pijssima regina ca
Camera dignissima Sal
    O clemens clement
    Adora filia virgini
    virgiñ laetitia sch
    Dei plena gratiae

Away w

Away with
twill make
the hap[i]e

the pocket t
no niggard s
A fobb that
I tell thee m
O hee neuer
to sweeten st

Away with tl
twill make vs
the hap[i]est

When monye
from whores
he smels to n
from milions
he saueth hims
he weares out

Away with this
twill make vs a
the hap[i]est a

Hee Cheateth
takes care for
remembers not
he sighneth no
away all is hurl
and all that hau

Away with this
twill make vs all
the hap[i]est ar

Aye me can love and bewtie soe conspire

Aye me
can love and bewtie soe conspire
to wronge the zeale of true desire.
aye me
can shee prove falce who wonte to sweare
& sacrifice her goulden hayre
aye me
breake harte in twaine
to end this paine
& while I dye
thus will I crye
aye me
noe more my flowre
noe more my rose thy falshood doth thy freends deflowre
aye me
thou wonst to be sweete loves delight
but now art wounded to dispighte
aye me
breake harte in twaine
to end this paine
and while I dye
thus will I crye
aye mee.

Ch.Ch.MS.439, ff.15ᵛ,16.

Be not proud, nor coye nor cruell

Be not proud, nor coye nor cruell
be more gentle, let me warne thee;
thinke not beautye such a Jewell,
but it maye fade, & men maye scorne thee;
gainst wch danger prithee Arme thee:
And loose noe tyme whylst thou Art younge,
at fifteene sweet staye not too longe.

Pinkes & violets in their tyme
for their sweetnes are Affected
beautyes growinge past their prime
soone are slighted & neglected
like fadeinge flowers Nought respected
then loose noe tyme whylst thou Art younge
At fifteene sweet staye not too longe.

let not thy beautye waste in vayne
loue whylst y^{t} thy Sum̃er lasteth
noe Aprill can reviue Againe
Anye beautye y^{t} once passeth
her Maye's pryde but stright it wasteth
then loose noe tyme whylst thou art younge
At fifteene sweet staye not too longe.

B.M.Loan MS.35,f.28^{v}.

Be not proud pritty one

Be not proud pritty one,
for I must loue thee,
thou art faire but vnkind
yet dost thou vse mee
Red ar thy lips & Cheeks
like too thy blushes
the flame thats in thyne Eye
burnes myne to Aishes

And on the brest
the place of loues abyding
sitts Cupid high Enthrond,
my paines deriding
O if a God thou art
wound her yt scornes mee
or fall from that bright spheare,
wch soe adornes thee.

Then might my sighs and teares
Moue her Compassion
And on her hart of Flint
Make some impression
knowing her bewty hath
Thus far ensnard mee
and all the Joyes of loue
haue stil debard mee

O Gentle loue thy frowne
Now would distroy mee
hauing livd but in hope
once to jnioye thee
And sure my death would
add nought to your Glorie
But rather all your fame
dye in the Storye.

B.M.Add.M S.31432, f.38.

27

Bee quick my Boyes drinKe off y^r wine

Bee quick my Boyes drinKe off y^r wine
Care but inslaues the Soule;
if want of that maKe you repine,
then Kisse this freindly bowle.

But as it Ebbs fill it with teares
to that Eclep[s]ed glorye,
thus tho wee may Not speaKe our feares,
healths shall repeate his story,
Next to our hopes though now wee bee
Expos'd to want & scorninge,
The Sunne y^{t's} sett in blood will bee
signe of a Joyfull morninge.

Bee quick my Boyes drinKe off y^r wine
Care but inslaues the Soule;
if want of that maKe you repine,
then Kisse this freindly bowle.

Hast then fayre light & with thy beames
Scatter thes Men of might
Or helpe vs with our Loyall streames
to drowne their stollen light
Soe shall thes Stateists that designe
Joy to their black desire
When thou breaK'st forth like Glowormes shine
W^{ch} if but touch'd Expire.

Beauty wch all Men admire

Beauty wch all Men admire
corrects and chastens my desire
pride and scorne ye servants are
yt vsher us vnto ye faire
and to so certeine losse wee run,
that though wee thrive wee are vndone,
Servile natures love them most
and but of bondage cannot boast,
love them still and live in scorne,
for such vile vse to vs they're borne.

Before the sonne had guilde the morne of silver daij

Before the sonne had guilde the morne of silver daij
I walkinge fownd wher one forlorne lamentinge laij
vnto his siges the powers aboue invoked hee
o marse o Joue o soll o loue howe faire is shee

weare those her eyes that I beheld o heavenlie dame
her feet the pillares that vphold soe right a frame
shee was a creture that did moue more like the spheare
of marse of Joue of sole of loue or one more faire

But o whie did shee wth her flight dishoner me
whie feard shee wronge wher nought but right could offerde be
I ment none other but to proue to praise or wooe
as mars or Joue or sole or loue inamored doe

I ment not what to thinke is synne her looke inchaunt
her features woode her fashions win wch let her graunt
and when I question her alone for modestee
let marse or Joue or sol or loue then punishe mee.

Might I but onlie fixed stand in her imbrace
wth lipes to intertaine her hand wth looke her face
bare I her traine weard I her gloue what cares I
though mars or Joue or sol or loue should punishe me

But since shee is a match for gode & not for men
I would her bewtie had suche odes would sel them then
that when their goulden septers stroue in mutiny
who might enuye her loue might fall to mee

What eū answeare shee replies vnto my loue
whiles mars wth Citherea lies wth Juno Joue
while sol in spangled signes aboue doe ride or shine
whiles Cupid is surnamed loue shee shalbe myne.

B.M.Add.MS.29481, f.15^v.

30

Begon thou fatall fyery feauer

Begon thou fatall fyery feauer
               let loue alone
wth his etheriall flames possess my brest :
his fiers wth thy consuming heate noe ayd requires
               but swift desires
transports my passions to a throne of rest
when I who in the pride of health did neuer feele such warmth to
    moue
by sickness tam'd am now inflamd I know no Joyes but loue
& he yt trifled many a tedious hower away my loue to try
in little space hath gaind ye grace to haue more power then I.

depart thou fatall fury from mee now depart
               thinke not my heart
to thy dull flames shall be a sacrifice
a maid dread Cupid now hath on thine alter layd
               by thee betraid
a rich oblation to restore thine eyes
but yet thy fore acknowledgment can testifye thou hadst no craft
to bend thy bow against a foe that aymes to catch thy shaft
nor doe I feare If at my brest all at once thy darts doe moue
she that receaues a thousand sheaues she can no more but loue
nor doe I feare if at my bosome all at once thy darts doe fly
he yt reseaues a thousand wounds he can no more but dye

No more phisitions let me tire youre braines no more
               praye giue me ore
I haue a cure in phisicke neuer reed
all though youre skillfull doctors all the world doth know
               pray let me goe
you may as men doe make practise on the dead
if my laceris daine to uiew me with the glory of his lookes
I shall not doubt to liue without phisitiones or theire bookes
tis he that with his balmy kisses can restore my latest breath
what bliss it is to gaine a kisse can raise a maid from death.

To you that tell me of another world I be
              & will alow
youre sacred precepts if you'le grant me this
that he whome I esteeme of next to deity
              may goe with me
without his presence there can be no bliss
goe teach youre tenants of eternity to those that a[n]gels be
doe not perswade a louesick maide theres any heauen but he
yet stay methinks an icye slumber doth possesse my phransie braine
pray bid him dye If you se I doe neuer wake againe

Drexel MS.4041,ff.46ᵛ-47ᵛ.

Behold Great Neptunes Risen from yᵉ deep

Behold Great Neptunes Risen from yᵉ deep,
wᵗʰ all his Tritons and begins to sweep
the Rugged waues into a smoother Forme,
not Leaueinge One small wrinckle of a Storme

Marke how yᵉ wynds stand still, & on her Gaze,
see how her Beautye doth yᵉ Fishe Amaze.
the whales haue Begd this Boone of wynde and weather,
that on their Backs they maye Convaye her hyther.

And See, shee lands, Just like yᵉ Ryseinge Sun,
that Leaues the Bryny Lake, when Night is done,
Flye Flye Amintor to thy Envyde bliss,
And let not Earth Rob thee of her First kiss.

B.M.Loan MS.35,ff.151,151ᵛ.

Beliza shade your shining eyes

Beliza shade your shining eyes,
for we that liue in lesser light
doe want a Glorious stock of Sight,
to Make to your bright lookes replyes.

Our Feeble lights to[o] smale to view,
loues Iurisdiction in your face,
wher snow and Corrall striue for place,
as yet Vnknowne to which his due,
And whilst we reconcile them ther,
Reflections wch your faire Eyes Make
distract us soe that we mistake,
and loose our Iudgments in our Feares.

Beliza shade your shining eyes,
for we that liue in lesser light
doe want a Glorious stock of Sight,
to Make to your bright lookes replyes.

With Essence of some powre devine
the God of loue doth your lookes fill
and all ar Captiues by free will
on whome soe Ere those glaunces shyne
Though by experience we Can proue
your Modesty will scarce admitt
to thinke Platonicke loue is fitt
yet from your Eyes, we feare to loue

Beliza shade your shining eyes,
for we that liue in lesser light
doe want a Glorious stock of Sight,
to Make to your bright lookes replyes.

The softest slackes of Gentler teares
we offer for a Sacrifice
to hange as Clowds betwixt your Eyes
and our addresses made in feares
And may our faith teach us to Vse
the fauours of your shyning beames
as we doe hopes in pleasing dreames
wch in our Waking we must loose

Beliza shade your shining eyes,
for we that liue in lesser light
doe want a Glorious stock of Sight,
To Make to your bright lookes replyes.

B.M.Add.MS.31432,ff.36ᵛ,37.

Bibamūs hilares

Bibamūs hilares
vinūm hispanicūm,
Nil tam jūcūndūm
aūt tam bonūm,
Quia laetificat
mentes hominūm,

venite alacres
nūnc bacchi milites,
seū mentes arma
satis fortia
Iūgate maestia
cordis agmina.

Pocūla dūm resonant
vacūa dūm resonant
       victoria.

Squyer MS.490.69.

Bid not farewell for fate can ne're divorce

Bid not farewell for fate can ne're divorce
two wedded soules those parts of earth in me
I have imprison'd in a Vestall course
by their restraint to set my best part free
Then cease adieu though part on earth we must
or soules shall meet w^n bodies turne to dust.

Tis not a cell or habit seekes to hide
Beauty or love or youth or elder age
But holy thoughts in humble minds y^t bide
To contemplate Lifes weary pilgrimage
This is y^t veile divides ye world & me
To crowne corruption wth eternity.

Bod. Lib.MS.Don.c.57,ff.50^v-1.

Blood thirsty care goe packe

Blood thirsty care goe packe
y^u enymy to health,
goe fill the misers lapp
y^t pynes amidst his wealth

no more of sorroes hy ho
Then but drinke we of the strongest
laugh & be fatt sing merryly
let him take all liues longest

what if thy nose looke red
shall ye body fare the worse
by drinke ye like is fed
though the plauge consume the purse

no more of sorroes hy ho
Then but drinke we of the strongest
laugh & be fatt sing merryly
let him take all liues longest

how scap'st thou gentle tinker,
when hang'd were 4 and twenty
he liues to be youre scinker
and drinke all ye potts empty

no more of sorroes hy ho
Then but drinke we of the strongest
laugh & be fatt sing merryly
let him take all liues longest.

Drexel MS.4041,ff.120-121^v.

Blow gently passion in my faire ones breast

Blow gently passion in my faire ones breast
breath out no rugged thoughts 'gainst one distrest
my anchord hopes seemes straynd feare too unkinde
foretells the shipwrack of a louesick minde
           Ay me I sink
            despaire my brink.

Blowe there sweet Zephirus where thou shalt finde

Blowe there sweet Zephirus where thou shalt finde
a breath more Aromaticke then thy winde,
when through the Arabian coast perfum'd it flyes
by spicye flames, in wch the Phoenix dyes.
Blowe there & ad vnto thy sweetnes store,
such as when she is not shall be noe more

Cauerne it vp, & keepe that Soueraigne breath
to purifye the Aire in tyme of death.
Blowe there & in soft language spoaken lowe
(thou gentle aire) in secrett make hir knowe
how like the Phoenix I doe sacrifize,
my hart to hir inflamed by hir Eyes.

Egerton MS.2013,ff.52ᵛ,53. and again ff.64ᵛ,65.

Breake Hart in twayne, fayre Ronile may se

Breake Hart in twayne, fayre Ronile may se
how much her Crueltye hath injurd thee ;
thy teares, & Sighes, soe powerles haue bin,
y^t laughter they from her, not pittye wiñ.
wert thou once deade tis like she would lament,
& seeme to sighe to shew som discontent,
not y^t she lou'de but to preserue her fame,
& shun ye Tytle of A Murdres Name.

B.M.Loan MS.35,f.12ᵛ.

Bright soule, Instruct poore Mortalls how to Mourne

Bright soule, Instruct poore Mortalls how to Mourne
How to approach yet not prophane thine Vrne
To come wth Humane sighes or Eyes,
were sure too bold a sacrifice,
least a foule teare, or Nauseous Gust,
should scatter Or defile thy dust.
wee should in homage to thy shrine,
weepe out our humor Christaline
which ther congeald might saphirs turne,
by borrowing Lustre from thine vrne
They onely Know such Losses to Condole
who can for euery sigh, breath out a Soule.

Bright Soule Instruct vs to that Just respect,
wth which thy Hallowed Ashes must bee decKt
To build them Trophies were vnjust,
thy vertues Canopye thy Dust
To write vpon them were not safe,
thy Name is thy best Epitaph
To carue thy statue were amisse,
thy BooKe thy best Colossus is
T'inclose thy Reliques were vneuen ;
Noe shrine is fitt for thee but heauen
Can Nothinge lend thee lustre May wee turne
Nothinge If Nothinge will adorne thine vrne.

HearKe HearK how Each Orbe his time doth Keepe
whilst Peales of Angells Ringe.
And since wee cannot fitly weepe
letts try how wee can singe
Since Charles aduanc't beyond the Kinge,
is plac't aboue his waine
'Twer sure a Sacrilegious thinge
to weepe him downe againe
Then lett our Accents all conspire
with Heauens lou'd Harmonye,
whilst this short Anthem fills ye Quire
Hee's welcome to ye sky.

By all thy Gloryes willingly I goe

By all thy Gloryes willingly I goe,
yet could haue wishd thee Constant in thy loue,
but since, thou Needes must proue,
vncertaine as is thy beautye,
or as ye glass yt showes it thee,
my hopes thus soone to Ouerthrow,
showes thee more fickle, but my flames by this,
are easier quencht then his,
whom flatt'ringe Smyles betraye?
'tis Tyrranous delaye
breeds all ye Harme,
& makes yt fyre Consume wch should but warme.

Till Tyme distroye those blossomes of thy youthe
thou art our Idoll worshipt at that Rate,
but whoe can tell thy fate
& saye that when this beauties done
this Louers Torch shall still burne On,
I could haue seru'de thee wth such truth
devoutest Pilgrims to their Saincts doe show
departed longe agoe,
And at thy Ebbinge tyde
haue vsde thee as a Bryde
whose only true
whylst you are fayre he loues himselfe, not you.

B.M.Loan MS.35,f.146ᵛ.

Can he yᵗ loves be man

Can he yᵗ loves be man,
When his Captain's but a Child?
for he that leades is wilde,
shall love be gag'd by th' spann,
Lovers say they are Kinde,
when their wordes and deedes are blinde.

Yf loves-lord want his eyes
and his subiects seekes to guide
must not the obayer slyde
ledd by his Lords disguise
Hee that obayes his check
followes him, to break his neck.

Care away goe thow from me

Care away goe thow from me,
for I am no fit match for thee -
Thow bereav'st me of my wits,
wherefor I hate thy frantick fits
Therefor I will care no more,
since that in cares comes no restore,
Būt I will sing hey doūn a doūn a dye,
and cast care away away from me.

If I want I care to gett
the more I have it doth me freet [*sic*]
have I much I care for more
the more I have I think me poor
doth greife my mind oppress
In wealth or woe find no redress
Therefore I'le care no more no more in vain
for care hath cost me meikle greif and pain

Is not this world a slipprey ball
and thinks men strainge to catch a fall
doth not the sea both ebb and flowe
and hath not fortoun a painted show
why should men take care or greife
since yt in care comes no releife
ther's non so wise but may be overthrown
the careless may reap what the carefull have sowen

Well then Learn to know thy selfe
and care not for this worldly pelf
whither thy estate be great or smale
give thanks to god what ere befall
so shalt thou live at ease
no hidden greif shall the[e] displease
Then mayst thow sing hei down and down a die
when thou hast cast all greif and Care for the. [from thee.]

Squyer MS.490.65,66.

Careles of loue & free from feares

Careles of loue & free from feares
I sate & Gazd on Stella's Eyes
thinkinge my reason or my yeares,
might keep me safe from all Surprize

But Loue y^t hath bin longe dispis'de
& made ye Baud to Others trust
findinge his deitye surpris'de
& changde into degenerate Lust.

Sum̃ond vp all his strength & pow're
makeinge her face his magazine
where virtues grace & beauties flowre
he plac'de his Godhead to redeeme

soe that too late, (alass) I finde
noe steeled Armour is of proofe
nor can the best resolued mynde
resist her beautye & her youth!

but yet ye ffollye to vntwist
that loueinge I deserue noe blame
were it not Atheisme to resist
where Gods themselues conspire her fame.

B.M.Loan MS.35,f.96.

47

Cast away those silkne clouds

Cast away those silkne clouds,
whose dull and Enuious darknes shrouds
those heaunlye twiñes, wch did appeer
a Constellation, bright & cleere
fairer then those lights wch straye,
in Cinthyas or Appolloes daye.

Carnation Mantles wch doe folde
and keep these tender plants from colde
I Envye you, would she let me
of th' Order of her garter be,
her Sacred Rytes I would maintayne
contemninge all Sainct Georges trayne.

B.M.Loan MS.35,f.47.

Cease not thou heavnly voiced glorious Creature

Cease not thou heavnly voiced glorious Creature
                of Divinest feature
though chilnesse damps my soule sent from thine eyes
                yet quickning flames arise
Let sweetly mix't cold poisning aire still sound
                through my benumed heart
whil'st those fire shooting starres againe it wound
                wth a 2 forked dart
Ah! Let me live in such well temp'red anguish
& never dy but so for ever Languish.

Seace ô seace this hum of greiveing

Seace ô seace this hum of greiveing,
since the cawse of it is liveing,
what is lost awakes true moane,
he for whom wee weepes not gon
he but shiftes his court is fleeted,
where his worth's are better greeted
passion should to reason yeeld,
when the dead hath wun the feild.

Cease, sorrow cease, & doe noe More torment

Cease, sorrow cease, & doe noe More torment
my wearied Soule that faine would take some rest,
b'inge Ouer Cloyde wth care & discontent
to[o] hard for feeble nature to degest ;
desolue these stormes and show 'tis in thy powre,
to yeild a wretched life one happye Howre.

B.M.Loan MS. 35,f.32.

Cease thy wishes gentle boy

Cease thy wishes gentle boy
blindnesse is no such annoy
had ye Gods but lent thee sight
thine Eyes would have dimm'd their light
Such a day gives beauty grace
had not night usurp't thy face

Cupid's selfe doth want his sight
Wandring in perpetuall night
And fates therefore blinded thee
If he dyes Cupid to be
And if 'twere not for my mother
Thou wert Cupid or his brother.

Bod.Lib.MS.Don.c.57, f.47.

Celia, thy Sweet Angels face

Celia, thy Sweet Angels face
may be cald a Heaunly place,
the whytnes of the starrye waye,
Nature did on thy forehead laye,
but thyne Eyes hath brightnes woñ,
not from starrs but from ye Sun,
the blushinge of the Morne
in thy Rosie cheeke is worne,
ye Musique of the Heau'nly sphaeres,
in thy soule meltinge voice Appeeres,
Happje were I, had I (like Atlass) grace
soe faire a Heau'n wthin myne Armes t'imbrace.

B.M.Loan MS.35,f.63ᵛ.

Celia turnes awaye her Eyes

Celia turnes awaye her Eyes,
yt my flames might not arise,
as if loue dwelt Only there
and my brest noe Mansion were
Or yt beautie Ads more fire
to loues growth then doth desire;
but in my hart loue doth proue,
he is soe much greater loue,
as fire is greater wher it doth Enflame,
then wher it faintly shines, & warmes ye same.

Caron oh caron come away

S[uppliant] : Caron oh caron come away
　　　　　　　why dost yu let mee call soe longe
　　　　　　　when time yu knowest for none will stay
　　　　　　　in wch thou dost mee double wrong

C[haron] 　: Ho ho wt hasty wight doth call
　　　　　　　say whence yu comest or whether wouldst yu goe
　　　　　　　nor caron nor his boat weare made for all
　　　　　　　that call for to bee wafted to & fro :
　　　　　　　did loue or honor send yee say
　　　　　　　if not then caron meanes to stay :

　　　S : O list to mee & I will tell
　　　　　　ye cause of my sad fate

　　　C : Goe on poore soule I heare thee well
　　　　　　& will thy woes Abate

　　　S : Thanks gentle caron C : one I say

　　　S : then truth to let thee know
　　　　　　twas loue him self sent mee this way

　　　C : that foolish Boy how soe

　　　S : by kilinge my poore heart wth greef
　　　　　　& wo[u]ndinge my sad soule

　　　C : & couldst thou then finde noe relife

　　　S : O noe C : Alas poore foole
　　　　　　this foolish wanton blind vnco[n]stant boy
　　　　　　doth send more soules vnto my boat & mee
　　　　　　then all the gods yt death doth still Imploy
　　　　　　on fatall destiny ye sisters three :

　　　S : oh hadst yu bene of human race
　　　　　　yu couldst not Breath forth such disgrace
　　　　　　of loue to hearm him foolish blynd
　　　　　　but wouldst haue borne a gentler mynd

C : weomen & fooles they are his subiects still
thowsands of such hee useth in ther kindes
he makes them whine & cry & sigh vntill
they bee as deafe & dumbe as hee is blynd
then laughfs at them & sends them tumbling hither
respecting them nor mee nor winde nor weather.

S : Caron I come I prethy hast away
my times prefixt I can noe longer stay

C : O heere I come S : thrice welcome now att last

C : then Come aboarde & to those pleasures hast
yt in Elizium growe S : For those I longe
and wish there still to liue. C : Then wth a song
in spite of loue as I do wafte thee thither
weell singe of ioyes & all delights together

S : then to those fields And most delightfull playnes
where louers gin there joyes & end there paynes.

Cloris I faine would try to love againe

Cloris I faine would try to love againe,
But thou hast so ill vsd me heretofore,
that though I shovld forgive thee all the paine
I sufferd yet tis hard to love thee more,

I covld forgive thee y^t thou thence might'st Know
ye vallew of thee wch my Heart did hold,
But shovld thy Pitty from y^t passion flowe
'twould more afflict me then thy scornes of old

'twould make my healed wounds againe fresh bleed,
Yet power thee out their pardon for my harmes
But Dead thoult find me drop downe at thy feet
that liveing never covld attayne thyne armes

Knowe then I love thee still and wish thine to,
But from the Knowledge of it begg repreive,
O this poore sovle of mine 'twould quite vndoe,
to Knowe thou pittyest now I cannot live,

Yet wilt thou when I am Dead but Kisse theise Bankes
of livid flesh in sorrow for disdaine
They from y^t warmth, shall then returne thee thankes
for him y^t would not live to Love againe.

Bod.Lib.MS.Mus.b.1, ff.171,171^v,172.

Cloris I wish that Envye were

Cloris I wish that Envye were
as Just as Pitty doth apeare
vnto your state that soe I might
Robb others to giue you delight,
but your to[o] free though louely Charme
in Others gloris brings you Harme,
for while you willingly admitt
soe Many Rivalls to your Witt
vnthriftily you throw away,
the pleasure of your bewtious sway,
wch loosely scattard soe on Many,
securely fastens not on any,
And soe your bewtye to discouer,
brings Many Gazers but noe Louer.
And your too Greedye hands distroy,
what you Would your selfe Injoye,
Soe Princes by Ambition Tristy Growne
in Chace of Many Kingdomes loose ther Owne.

B.M.Add.MS.31432,ff.45,45ᵛ.

Cloris, since my death doth com from you

Cloris, since my death doth com from you,
O repaire vnto my Tombe, & veiw
ye Marble yt does hyde me, & from that,
deriue ye Cruell storye of my fate :
first, when my figure thou hast found,
devoutly kneeling on ye ground,
as if it prayde thinke it me,
whoe still Am worshiping of thee ;
& if noe dolefull sound Approach thyne Eare,
to testifye a passion nor a teare
fall from myne Eye doe not beleiue I'me dead,
but to that statue Metamorphosed,
then, then giue a sighe, & in thy hart bemoane,
him whom thyne Eyes Converted to A stone.

B.M.Loan MS.35,f.80ᵛ.

Cloris when I to thee present

Cloris when I to thee present,
ye cause of all my discontent
And show how all ye wealth that can
flow from this little world of man,
is nought but Constancy and loue
why will you Other Objects proue.

O doe not Cousen yor desires
wth Comon or Michañick fyres
that Lustre wch you See in golde
in Eury shop is to be solde
And Diamonds of Richest prize
men Only valew wth their Eyes.

but looke vppon my Loyall hart
that knowes to vallew Eury part
And loues thy hydden virtues more
then Outward shapes wch fooles Adore
in that you'le all ye treasure fynde
that can Content a noble mynde.

B.M.Loan MS.35,f.146.

Close by a fringed Banke I found

Close by a fringed Banke I found
   stretch'd on ye Grovnd
   a Sheapheard swaine,
the list'ning waters wch ran nigh
   swell'd by his eye
   sadly complain'd
ye fond youth's fate, and in his groanes
shar'd as partakers of his moanes,

Cloris (quoth hee) these purling streames
   may prove apt theames
   for love to thee
they if but woo'd with ha[l]fe theise teares
   would drowne my feares,
   and set me free,
but thou'rt more mercilesse by farre,
then swelling seas or rivers are

Th'amorous Turtles at my plaint
   growe strang'ly quaint
   and finding you
so cruell and vniust
   themselves mistrust
   as guilty too,
and each doth from his fellow fly
corrupted by thy tyranny,

The Lyon yet and Panther wilde,
   are both growne milde,
   and vnto me
doe proffer more vnfained Love
   then sighs covld move
   or begg from thee,
if then my sighs have power to swage
the savage beast's why not thy rage,

Noe Cloris noe thy stony brest
        forbids all rest,
        and tis in vaine
this fatall houre shall soone fullfill
        thy cruell will,
        and end my paine
wch said Hard Harted Maide he cry'd
farewell oh farewell oh farewell and so dy'd.

Bod.Lib.MS.Mus.b.1,ff.114ᵛ,115,115ᵛ,116.

Cold Heritique &

Cold Heritique &

. . . .

Hast thou taKen Poppy seed
Hemlock or the Mandrake weed ?
Or hast thou deriu'd this Curse
from thy Mother or thy Nurse
Say what distemper of thy Blood,
MaKes thee resist the Common Good
Thou y^t enamourd of Anoy,
Lou'st but to sue, Not enjoy
Pursue thy foolish hopes & feares,
picke the Soft waxx out her eares

. . . .

Begg a Teare, if thou bee dry
Or sucke ye Rheum out of her eye
Aske a fruitless dreame instead
of a lusty Maydenhead

. . . .

feele her Elbowes for her Hipps,
Loue her when thou art a sleepe
WaKeinge from those follyes weepe,
Doate vppon her Midnight breath,
and enjoy her after death,
Pray Idoliter in vaine
varye all thy hopes wth paine,
& from mee receiue this Curse
Mallice hath not found a Worse.

Edinburgh Univ.Lib.MS.Dc.1.69.38-40.

Collen say why sittst thou soe

Strephon : Collen say why sittst thou soe,
　　　　　　crossed Armes are signes of woe
　　　　　　If thy Nymph noe fauour show,
　　　　　　Choose another lett her goe
　　　　　　for here are store, as sweet,
　　　　　　as smooth, as white, as fayre
　　　　　　as gentle too & debonaire

Collen　　 : Strephon peace thou dost prophane
　　　　　　Neuer yet vppon this plaine,
　　　　　　Such perfections haue bin seene
　　　　　　as adorne my fancy's Queene
　　　　　　Neuer none soe fayre soe bright
　　　　　　None soe rosye, none so white.

Chorus　　 : Neuer none soe fayre soe bright
　　　　　　None soe rosye, none so white.

Strephon : Though shee cheefe perfections haue
　　　　　　yett shee flyes when thou dost craue,
　　　　　　But a Smile thy life to Saue
　　　　　　And thy Loue procures a graue.
　　　　　　Then change thy minde Loue one,
　　　　　　as smooth as white, as fayre,
　　　　　　More Kinde then shee, more debonaire.

Collen　　 : E're I leaue Corella's Loue
　　　　　　Though shee still more cruell proue
　　　　　　May the Suñ forbeare to shine
　　　　　　Wher I am, or ought of mine
　　　　　　May the Wolfe or Tyger bee
　　　　　　Ruine to my flocks & mee

Chorus　　 : This poore Collen weepinge sayd
　　　　　　whilst his flocks neglected stray'd.

64

Com, com sad Turtle Mateles Moaninge

Com, com sad Turtle Mateles Moaninge,
droop noe more for want of Oweninge!
heres a brest, for yor Nest,
Like an Alter Cypress-drest.
Sacrificeinge greif-full groaninge.
Com Sad Turtle O com Hyther
our fates Alike, let's dye together!

Com, Com & vse sighe soothinge skill
& wth Cooinge gently kill,
soone as Aspes fatall Claspes,
whylst yor sad, glad feeder gaspes,
feed on woe & feast yor fill.
Com sad Turtle O com Hyther
our fates Alike, let's dye together!

B.M.Loan MS.35,f.56.

Come come sweet Love why dost y^u stay

Come come sweet Love why dost y^u stay
come let us meet ere envious day
draw back ye curtaines of ye night
hindring harmlesse loves delight.
come quickly come make no delay
lets take o^r pleasure while we may.

Come drawer some wine or wele pull downe your Signe

Come drawer some wine or wele pull downe your Signe
for wee are all Souell compounders
wele make the house ringe with healths to ye king
& confusion unto his Confounders.

Since goldsmiths Committye affords us no pitty
our sorrowes in wine we will step⌢vm
they forst vs to take to oaths & we make
a third that we nere meane to keepe⌢vm

And first who ere sees wele drink on our knees
to the king may thay Choake yt repine
a fig for the trators yt looke to his waters
they haue no thing to doe with our wine

And next heers A cup to ye queene fill itt vp
wert poyson we would make an end ont,
may charles & she meete & tread one yr feete
both presbiter & independant

To the prince & all others his sisters & brothers
as low in Condition as high borne
wee drinke this & pray yt shortly they may
se all those yt rongd them at Tiburne

And now heers 3 bowles to all gallant soules
yt for ye king die and will venter
may thay flowrish when those who are his & yr foe
are dambd and ramd downe to the Center

And last lett a glase to our vndoers passe
attendended [sic] with to or 3 Curses
may plauges sent from hell stuffe yr bodies as well
as Caualeirs quine does there purses

May the Canne balls of pimm eat⌒em vp lim by limm
or a feauer scortch them to Embers
pox keepe vm in bed vntell they are dead
or Compound for the losse of there members

And may they be found in nought to abound
but heauens and there Countries anger
may they neuer want fractions douts feares & distractions
till the gallow tree take them from danger.

Drexel MS.4041,f.122'.,122ᵛ.

Come heauy hart, whose sighs thy Sorrowes shew

1.   Come heauy hart, whose sighs thy Sorrowes shew
         and let us be partakers of thy woe
         who did thee wound Confess and not denye,

2.   An Arrowe headed with a Womans Eye,

1.   Those darts are wont to wound & hitt,
         yet tend the place wher bewty Vse to sitt.

2.   But when loue shoots them, then they fly wth force
         and hitt, and wound, and kill without remorce.

1.   loues blind and sees noe shaft, wch way it flyes,

2.   but all his Arrowheads, are woemens Eyes.

1&2   What shall we doe to be reuendge on loue

1.   ther is but one way 2. And the same weele proue.

1&2   And the same weele proue
         Weel steale his Arrowes And will head them New
         with weomens harts And then theyl neare fly true.

B.M.Add.MS.31432,ff.26ᵛ,27.

Come lusty ladyes come come wth pensiue thought℮ ye pyne

Come lusty ladyes come come wth pensiue thought℮ ye pyne
come learne the galliard now at vs for we be maskers
we singe we dance & we reioyce wth myrth in modesty
come Ladyes then and take a pte & as we singe daunce yee
& farre ran tā tā tā tā tararan tyna.

Ch.Ch.MS.439,ff.28ᵛ,29.

Come my Oenone Lett us doe

Paris   : Come my Oenone Lett us doe
             yt wch ye spring invites us to
             Lett us sleepe & dreame & kisse
             there is sweet delight in this
             ye fleecy flocke yt bleating graze
             can only see not blabb or playes

Oenone : First to thy browes I here bequeath
             this Lylly rosy-mixed wreath
             Now Letts hye us to ye bowres
             where weele sport us under flowres
             keepe but yie promis'd vowes & nights
             & weele teach Venus new delights

Paris   : Ere I prove false Zant shall forsake
             his forward course & backeward take
             & Nilus shall forgett to know
             ye season of his overflow

Oenone : The nipping north shall breath no frost
             & Tagus golden sand be Lost
             yn shall sweet Hybla want a bee
             ere yie Oenone falls from thee

Paris &
Oenone : Thus time & truth shall justify & prove
             the faith of Paris & Oenones Love.

Bod.Lib.MS.Don.c.57,ff.11v-12v.

Come Sorrow wrap me in thy sable cloake

Come Sorrow wrap me in thy sable cloake
& weigh my heart downe wth thy Leaden hand
Come presse my braine & from my eyes provoke
unliquid teares y^t on my cheekes may stand
Like dropps of gumm for ever Let me groape
in darke dispaire & finde no glimpse of hope
For she is dead Oh greife wch dost containe
more weight y^n all ye world Crush out my soule
y^t she Deare she & I may meet againe
Nor shall ye Iron fates my vowes controule
for she is dead thus thus poore Amantas spake
y^n cryd againe she's deade & his heart brake.

Come take a Carouse

Come take a Carouse
weare Lords of the House,
our Spiritts are now high flown a
the steward is right
and a figg for the knight,
his whore and his treasurs our owne a

Then drink and be merry,
weele haue a figary,
and tast all sorts of pleasure,
he y^t slipps by [the] Cupp
and drinks not all upp,
deserues nor the whore nor the treasure.

B.M.Add.MS.31432,f.18.

Come Vyolle come Lett me thy necke embrace

Come Vyolle come Lett me thy necke embrace
To my sad treble sound a dolefull Base
helpe me to mourne since mirth is banisht quite
& clearest day turn'd into dismall night
helpe me to mourne wth thy well tuned strings
sith Love in sorrow sorrow in Love sings.

Cruell Clarinda tell me why

Cruell Clarinda tell me why
thou scornst thus in disguise?
that murder in thy Heart shovld lye,
when Love lyes in thine Eyes?
Why like a Syren falce and faire
thou do'st poore Soules betray,
And tak'st us Prisoners in thy Haire
letting none scape away.

Bod.Lib.MS.Mus.b.1,f.173ᵛ.

Cupid blushes to behold

Cupid blushes to behold
that yor bloods ar grown soe cold
& his wanton Mother sweares
yee'r a Scandall to yor yeares
reuiue youthfull fires then
& redeeme yor names agen
Banquet & the lusty wine,
beauty musick all Combine
wth quick spirits lofty straines
to put new life into your veynes
who then is dull when loue thus striues to please
damne him kind Nature to ye want of these.

B.M.Add.MS.10338,ff.36ᵛ-38.

Cupid if thou tell-tale prove

Cupid if thou tell-tale prove,
and publish I am now in Love
I will undoe thy power and thee
sweareing it was not thy device,
thy flashes could not thaw ye ice
that cristalls ore my chastety,

thy golden shafft's vnhealthfull found
yt cannot peirce without a wound
the God of Love is nectar now
my lipps and cheekes with this are dy'd,
and haue their blushes deifyed.
This is more potent then thy Bow,

But Love if thou no blabb wilt bee,
my breath shall kindle fire for thee,
yt shall inflame ye Northerne starr
I'll teach thine arrowes with mine eye
to drill a Marble as they fly
yet leaue no weeping wound nor scarre,

but if thy silence thus I cannot winne
tell on, I love a God, and that's no Sinn.

Bod.Lib.MS.Mus.b.1,ff.112ᵛ,113.

Cupids wearie of the Court

Cupids wearie of the Court
for Vertue ther hath spoild my sport
In that Cold Clyme I Canot Liue,
nor for that frozen zone doe Care,
wher Ladyes all platonick Are,
Some Other Region I must proue,
tis heresye, Grand Heresye in loue,
to be all Contemplatiue,
With my Quiuer and my Bowe,
Ile to the Actiue Citty Goe,
wth my quiuer and my Bowe,
Ile to the Actiue Citty goe.

Cupid my Mris hart assaild

Cupid my Mris hart assaild,
but neither force, nor craft availd,
thence he retreited In her eyes
to lurke while he advantge spies,
where now in Amboosh he doth lye
to gaine her heart, or there to dye.

Cupid thou Art A sluggish boye

Cupid thou Art A sluggish boye
& doost neglect thy callinge
thy bow and Arrowes are a Toye,
thy Monarchye is fallinge
vnless thou doost recall thy selfe,
and take thy tooles about thee?
thou wilt be scornd by Eury Elfe
& all ye world will flout thee.
Rouze vp thy spirits be still a God
& play the Archer finely,
let none Escape thy shafte or Rod,
gainst thee haue spoke vnkindly
Soe mayst thou chance to plague y^t hart,
that Cruelly hath made myne smart.

B.M.Loan MS.35,f.33^v.

Daphnis came on a somers day

Daphnis came on a somers day
where fayrie phillis sleepinge lay
with brest halfe naked bare
he ran & gathered store of lillies
where wth hee covered his faire phillis
Shee beinge nought aware
fond boy why dost thow marr
those lillie bowrs & loose the paine
her Lillie brest doth staine
all flowres & lillies farr :

Ch.Ch.MS.439,f.11ᵛ.

Deere my deere why are you cruell

Deere my deere why are you cruell :
to your more then wretched triall
ffeedinge fire of skorne wth fuell :
oyld wth bewties Sweetest Galle
when I doe thinke how I am wounded
with the Eye that I adore
then I sighe and am confounded
where I sought Salve for my Sore.

Sighes or teares could they move pittie :
or the pale badge of my woe :
Ør weare hate not cruell wittie :
would it lett me languish soe :
Noe alas the spight created :
In the tiger robd of younge :
When my Sighe would be abated
fayninge gentlye on my Songe.

Ch.Ch.MS.439,f.10^v.

Deare Venus, if thou wilt bee Kinde

Deare Venus, if thou wilt bee Kinde,
trust mee wth beautye for an howre :
the Comon-wealth of Loue shall finde,
How sweetly I will vse my pow'r.

Or let vs all bee fayre by turne
such a relation would restraine
The Tyrannie of femall scorne
least Wronge should bee return'd againe

for that wee Louers Mourne, & pine
This endless Empire is the cause,
the Poore haue Bountie in designe
And subjects still reforme ye Lawes

But if noe Hope for injur'd Men
of Comfort, Or release ther bee,
wee'le rise & Leuell Beautie then
And make a perfect Anarchie

B.M.Add.MS.29396,ff.64ᵛ,65.

83

Dearest all faire is in your browne

Dearest all faire is in your browne,
smyles are not smoother then your frowne.
Red is to[o] feavorish and the white,
growes sickly pale and Coole at night,
Such bewtys fades as soone as blowne,
and once enjoyed their sweets are Gone
But in thy Cheekes such Collers moue,
as makes the louer still to loue.

Not that I meane you want such white
More purer then the Mornings light
Or that your Chrimsone sweeters growes
then the New blowing DaMaske rose.
But that heere Nature shewing Art
as if it spoke in Euerie part
Mixing the Browne, blacke, white and Red
as wth rich Vailes EnCanoped

Shadowes are bewtyes Ornament
like to the Azure Firmament
wher Phebus shynes wher stars ar sett
as Dymonds caysd in blackest Jett
Making them shew in foyles being plact
more faire then by their Nature gract
like to a Goddesse in a shrowd
or the starrs breaking through a Clowd

O say not then I Canot place
thy loue on such a houghty face
tis Vertues Guise to lessen Most
those bewtyes wch themselues will boast
But I forgiue thee that beleeue
thou art the spheare wherin I liue
Nor Can I wish a blessing More
then being yours I soe adore.

B.M.Add.MS.31432,f.37ᵛ.

deere turne awaye thyne Eyes soe bright

deere turne awaye thyne Eyes soe bright,
such lightninges dazzle doe my Syght :
whose powrefull flames wthin are felt,
like founded gould my hart doth Melt.
& let me heer yt Heau'nly voice,
wch for to heer Angels rejoyce ;
since in the world what may Compare
A loulye Mayde as Chaste as fayre.

Death cañot yet Extinguish that entyre

Death cañot yet Extinguish that entyre
pure flame her Eyes did kindle in my brest ;
now they are clos'de & she is layde to Rest,
my hart hath Embers lefte of chaste desyre,
wch as the Elements soe they require
somthinge to feed & keep aliue the rest,
that hart, in wch her Image was Exprest,
shalbe the fuell, sight shall blow the fyre !
there now she seemes to move her sweetest lips,
wch Euer must be soe till they be none?
bids me not greiue? shee's but Ecclipsde
whoe from ye Eyes, not from ye hart is gone,
yet wth myne Eyes my hart shall beare a parte,
because myne Eyes first brought her to my hart.

B.M.Loan MS.35,ff.45,45ᵛ.

disdaine me not sweet loue though I be Ould

disdaine me not sweet loue though I be Ould,
greene is my loue all though my hayres be graye,
     nor am I Coulde,
noe matter what ye younge men saye,
I haue my blood as Hot, as red as they.

I am not wau'ringe, Constant is my Mynde
younge am I in desire, though Ould in yeares
     Selina prooue
my brest yt alway's vertue beares
to make both thyne and myne seeme golden Hair's.

B.M.Loan MS.35,f.10ᵛ.

87

Doe you not wonder at the strange rare sound

Doe you not wonder at the strange rare sound
wch doth from this Theorbo gravely rise,
That all yor Sences are as Captiues bound
yet pleas'd, With this soe sudden a surprize,
Ile tell you how it Comes, by Magick Art,
Tis strung wth fibres of my Mris Hart,
Where now it Lyes wthin this Hallowed womb;
to it a Sacred Piramide & Toomb;
Which shee can waken, when shee please to rise
A Greater wonder to your Eares & eyes.

Bod.Lib.MS.Mus.b.1,ff.85ᵛ,86.

Doris, See the Amorous flame

Doris, See the Amorous flame
how it Courts thy Noble Name
beckning sometymes with desire,
to th'embraces of the fyre
and then Gently Fañs aGen,
the Cleere storie of your Pen
As not Able to withstand,
the strickt bewtye of your hand
but Ambitious to Adore,
Rose to kisse and durst noe More.
Let not then the sencelesse flame
my deuoter seruice shame
yeild as much to my desire,
as thou Gau'st vnto the fyre
O Let mee Veiw it, though it turne,
mee to those Aishes you Would burne,
Soe shall your hand with my hart haue
a Willing and a freindly Graue.

B.M.Add.MS.31432,ff.46,46ᵛ.

downe downe afflicted soule and paie thy due

downe downe afflicted soule and paie thy due
to death & misserie, weepe howle & rue
the cryinge sines posest thee endles night
must euer lastlinglie hange ore thi hed
thy curst & guiltie Conscienc full of fright
distrust dispaire & torment for thy bed,
o thow must dye thow painted foole
wth all thy glori to the earth thou must
& all thi bewtie into dust
now ring thy knell
      dyng dong bell
      dinge dong bell.

B.M.Add.MS.29481, f.16.

90

Downe in a dale satt a Nimph weeping

Downe in a dale satt a Nimph weeping,
a Louely swayne satt by her sleepeing
shee Jogg'd and Joggd to haue him wake,
hee hunch't & punch't and nothing spake,
shee gaue him twenty & twenty kisses,
beeside her sighes and amorous wishes,
till eccho from hir plaints did chide him,
wch made him wake & runne to hide him,
In a pleasãnt thickett by,
after him ye Nimph did hie,
And for his Churlishnes beefore,
hee pleas'd her soe, shee cry'd noe more.

Fitzwilliam MS.52D, ff. 115ᵛ,116.

Downe in a vale there satt a shepherdesse

Downe in a vale there satt a shepherdesse,
bewailinge to her selfe her greate distress,
her downecast head, vpon her knee shee leante,
whilst with her hands her Curled haire she rent,
which careless lye, nowe hunge about her eares,
and only Seru'd her soe to dry her teares.

Her tears y^t from her red swolne eyes did flow,
faster then fountaines from there rivers goe,
her brest did heaue, as though her hart strings straynd,
each part exprest the Sorrowe shee Sustain'd,
only her tonge, her sorrowes were soe many
that it founde want of wordes to vtter any.

But by her face & Jesture was exprest
the liuely Image of a Soule distrest.

Fitzwilliam MS.52D,f.108^v.

Downe too farre usurping day

Downe too farre usurping day
ye bridegroome longs wth Love to play
night is Lovers Holy day
weep not faire maide yt names decay
weep no more but singing say
Hymen Hymen come away.

Phoebus drownes his golden ray
And shutts his light in evening gray
No longer now no longer stay
Weep then faire Maide yor long delay
Weepe yet weeping sing & say
Hymen Hymen come away.

England! once Europs envye now her scorne

England! once Europs envye now her scorne,
Ambitious to bee forlorne,
selfe by selfe torne,
stand amaz'd,
thy woes are blaz'd,
by sylence best,
& wanting words,
Ev'n wonder out ye rest.

Help gracious Kinge,
ye Sourze & springe,
of all or weale & bliss,
Alass ye faults not his,
Good Prince, to be mistooke,
how is hee greiu'd
or what's a Curse
far worse,
yt hee is not beleiu'd.

Help long wisht for Parliament,
if so good bee yor intent,
& will
& skill
why ill is or success.
Alass, Malignant Humors lurke
& 'cause ye Phisick cannot worke,
to giue or Woes redress.

Help in Law, ye Learned Sages,
studdied well in former ages,
but alass! our Rents
are beyond all precedents.
In fight
what's might,
yts right,
Statuts are over-aw'd,
& Comon Law, by Comon Law outlaw'd.

94

Help ye Divines, or Soares to playster,
settle ye Legacy wch your Master
bequeathed his owne, at his decease,
Ev'n peace.
Alass, alass, in Gilead
ther's noe Balme for to be had,
O Cruell!
they yt should holy water bringe,
Bringe fyre & fuell.

Noe help, Noe help, why then 'tis Vayne
for to Complayne.
(& why) Men syñ wth all their hart,
& sorrow wth but a part,
& all men Crye,
yt all is ill,
yet all doe seeke
to mak't or keep't
so still.

See'ng then or wounds are growne so wilde,
& all healpe try'de,
& all deny'de,
good god helpe vs at last,
before all helpe bee past,
for this is sure,
Man made these wounds,
but God alone can Cure.

B.M. Add.MS.11608, ff.4ᵛ-6ᵛ.

Excellent Mistresse fairer yn ye Moone

Excellent Mistresse fairer yn ye Moone
yn scowred pewter or a silver spoone
fairer yn Venus or ye Morning starre
dainty fine Mistresse by my troth you are
As farr excelling all ye other Nymphs
as Lobsters Crayfish or Crayfish Shrimps
yn glowormes bright your eyes doe shine more clearely
As I hope to be knighted I Love you most dearely
By my duodym [diadem?] halfe daggar I Love you most dearly.

Eyes gaze no more as yet you may

Eyes gaze no more as yet you may
in time forbeare, but yf you stay
& linger on allthough you would
you will forgett to be contrould
And let in such hott glowing beames
as quench you can not wth yr streames,
yf you would weep, as many teares,
as I haue seene both hopes and feares

Ch.Ch.MS.Mus.87,f.9v.

Eyes lie awake in hope of happy seinge

Eyes lie awake in hope of happy seinge
hope thought good hap was over longe in lingeringe
In comes the lasse of my thrice happy beinge
my hands thought longe vntill they weare a fingeringe
Loue Stood amazd respectiue of her honor
pittie saide holde but courage cryd vpon her.

Eies look off theires no beeholdinge

Eies look of[f] theires no beeholdinge
where is no obtayninge
what preuailes ye hartes vnfoldinge
and no hopes remayninge

Joyes y^t may not bee aspiered
wch no merritt can implore
when they are in vayne desiered,
doe but vex the minde the more

Close thyne eies and looke no longer,
wher the light confoundeth,
so the more and so the stronger
your desyer aboundeth

Damned soules rage discontented,
not so muche theire paynes to bide,
when they lye in hell tormented
as to haue theire heauen denyede

Tenbury Wells MS.1018,f.44^v.

ffaine I would but Ø I dare not

ffaine I would but Ø I dare not :
speake my thoughts at full to prayse her :
Speake the best cryes love and spare not :
thy speech can noe higher rayse her
Thy speech then thy thoughte is lower
yet thy thoughts doth not halfe knowe her.

Prayse I would but Ø how can I :
prayse her minde her bodye whether :
prayse them both cryes love If any :
for best is Shee alltogeether
Thy speech then thy thoughte is lower
yet thy thoughts doth not halfe knowe her.

Ch.Ch.MS.439,f.11.

Faine would I chang my maiden life

Faine would I chang my maiden life
and tast of loues true Joyes
what cange wouldest wishe to be a wife
maides wishes are but toyes
o can there be a greater wrong
then live a maide so longe
to church ringe out the marriage bell
ding dong ding dong ding dong.

Before that fiftene yeares where spent
I knewe on[e] have a sonne
how oulde art thow, sixteene come lent
alas wee are both vndone
o can there bee greater wrong
then live a maide so longe
to church ringe out the marriage bell
ding dong ding dong ding dong.

Ønce I hearde an oulde wife Hall [tell?]
how they that maidens die
what must they doe, lead apes in hell
a dolfull destinye
o wee will leade noe apes in hell
wee will change our maidens songe
wee will nether stay for church nor bell
wee have lived true maides to[o] longe

Tenbury Wells MS.1018, f.46ᵛ.

faine would I Cloris (Ere I dye)

faine would I Cloris (Ere I dye)
bequeath you such a Legacye;
as you might saye when I Am gon,
none has ye like; my hart Alone
were ye best guift I could bestow,
but yts already yors you know,
soe yt till you my hart Resigne,
or fill wth yors ye place of myne,
& by yt grace my store renew;
I shall haue nought worth giuinge you,
whose brest hath all ye wealth I haue,
saue a faint Carkas & a graue;
but had I as many hartes as haires
as many loues, as Loue has feares;
as many liues as yeares haue Howres;
they should be all, & Only yours.

B.M.Loan MS.35,f.56ᵛ.

ffaire and scornefull doe thy worst

ffaire and scornefull doe thy worst
I can laugh vntill I burst,
thou canst not breede me soe much care,
as to blanche or change a haire,
I cannot whine I cannot crye
nor putt ye finger in ye Eye;
but I can scowle & looke askewe,
and I can scorne as well as you,
faire & scornfull doe thie worst,
I can laugh—vntill thou burst.

Egerton MS.2013,f.41ᵛ.

faire Archibella to thine eyes

faire Archibella to thine eyes
yt paint iust blush on ye Skyes
each noble hart doth sacrifice
yet be not cruell cause you May
when ere you please or saue or slay
and with A froune beenight the day.

I doe not begg that you may rest
in an infected highway breast
ye lodging of each common guest
But I present A bleding hart
yt neuer knew A former smart
wounded by loue not prict by art.

be plesd to smile and then j liue
but if you frowne a death you giue
in which it were a sin to greiue
but if it be decreed j fall
grant yet one bone one boone is all
that you will me youre martir call.

Drexel MS.4041,ff.34-34ᵛ.

ffaire eyes regard my loue soe truelie tryed

ffaire eyes regard my loue soe truelie tryed
and let my truth be now at length rewarded
since it approves the worde wch never lyed
though vnbeeleefe would have my love discarded.

ffaire will you then that I shall dye

ffaire will you then that I shall dye,
O can soe beautifull an Eye,
vnto such cruelty incline,
as for your loue to lett me pine,
yf soe lett not thos Cometts shine

Deare rather with a sweet aspect
lett those cleare lamps their Rayes reflect
on him whose zeale is to thee more
then theirs that doe the sun adore
O lett those looks my life restore

But I alas to Death design'd
Condemne not thee though to[o] vnkind
since Destiny doth soe Ordaine
thy loue shall not my life susteine
Death is lesse Dismall then Disdaine.

B.M.Eg.MS.2013,f.61.

Fairest Theina let me know

Fairest Theina let me know
why still abroad yᵘ vailed goe,
Will not yʳ brighter face admit
yᵗ lights vnstrain'd should mixe with it?
Or doe yᵘ feare the Suns warme Kisse,
Alas yʳ owne burne more then his,
and we shall sooner find it trve,
The Sun will Sun burnt prove by you.

Strange that yoʳ vaile remains intyre
vntinderd yet my Heart on fire
But your bright Cristall eye may bee
vnalter'd though it alter'd mee,
As wee the Burneing glass behold
transfuse the Heart yet still be cold
Wᶜʰ wonder nothing elce can doe
Save heat begetting light and you;

But tis yoʳ pittyes art & prayse
to hide and break those peirceing rayse
which irrefract if they shovld shine
would strike amazement as devine
And wee for such a fond desire
Like semele consume in fire
Then give me leave you vail'd to love
least my Desire shovld fatall prove.

Faith be noe longer Coy

Faith be noe longer Coy
    but lets injoye
whats by the world Confest
    woemen loue best,
thy bewty fresh as may
    will soone decay,
besides within a yeare or too,
I shall be old and Canott doe.

Dost thinke that Nature Can
    for euerie Man
(had she more skill) provide
    soe faire a bride
Who euer Made a feast
    for a single guest
Noe without doubt she did intend
to serve thy Husband and his freind

To be a little Nice
    sets better price
On Virgins, and improoues
    ther servants loues
But on thy riper yeares
    it ill appeares
After a while youll fynde this true
I neede prouoking more then you.

B.M.Add.MS.31432,f.14ᵛ.

falce loue awaye, & all my sighes send back

falce loue awaye, & all my sighes send back
& fruitles tears in vayne shed for thy sake ;
& if soe be a messenger thou lack,
ye fame of thy falce fayth yt paines will take ;
yet though yt never any
soe falce there was of many,
for Charrity Ile tell to No-man,
whither thou art Man or woman !
only thus much I will make knowne to all ;
thou art a Creature aptest made to fall.

Farewell all future hopes y^t guide ye course

Farewell all future hopes y^t guide ye course
of fond conceites y^t never further goe
for fate or fortune ever make divorce
twixt me & mine fone [fare?] more y^n death can doe
for death divides but I y^t once must pt
body & soul but this rejoines ye heart

Farewell ye blisse of youth love's morning Starre
Where all amazing beames made nature proud
Adieu ye Starr of Beauty most divine
Eclip'st too soone by selfe-assumed cloud
Adieu all pleasure since a veile now hides
Beauty, Love, youth, & graces all besides.

Bod.Lib.MS.Don.c.57,f.50^v.

ffarewell deere infante Sucke ffrom my pensive brest

ffarewell deere infante Sucke ffrom my pensive brest
my life my harte my soule and lett me dye
wth thee alas wth thee my soule shall rest
that els wth greife in torments still shall lye
o lett the greatnes of my teares
and sighes even from my smarte
Imprinte pdigivs feares
wthin the tirants harte
that hee all grevous hellish sorrows may sustaine
and ever be repaide a thowsand times the like againe.

Ch.Ch.MS.439,ff.16ᵛ,17.

fill fill yᵉ bowele yᵉ lusty wyne will dye

fill fill yᵉ bowele yᵉ lusty wyne will dye
its Culler gins to fade
tis soe spritly soe deuine drinking
aught to bee a trade

tosse yᵉ glas
too thy las
drink itt of[f] boldly
hees an asse
lets it pas
hele fight but coldly.

for whn the canon thunders deth
and the surlye drums rezound
wine giues fainting sogers breth
cowerds faeres are in it dround,

tosse yᵉ glas
too thy las
drink itt of[f] boldly
hees an asse
lets it pas
hele fight but coldly.

the corpral yᵗ in belt of mach
wares his dredfull puyzant blade
suping this in hutt of thatch
yᵉ diuel cannot make afrade

tosse yᵉ glas
too thy las
drink itt of[f] boldly
hees an asse
lets it pas
hele fight but coldly.

hee that will not take this Cup
shuer a coward base must bee
sence ye virtue of this sup
giues asured victory,

tosse ye glas
too thy las
drink it of[f] boldly
hees an asse
lets it pas
hele fight but coldly.

Flow my teares fau from yor Springs

Flow my teares fau from yor Springs
exilde for ever Let me morne
where nights black birde her sad Infamy singes
there let me live ffor Lorne.
Never may my woes be Releeved
since pittie is ffled
& teares & sighes & grones my wery dayes,
of all Joyes have deprived
Harke you shadowes that In darknes dwells
learne to contēne Lighte
Happy happy they that in Hell
ffeeles not the worlds despight.

Downe vaine Lights shine you noe more
noe nights are darke enoughe ffor those
That in dispaire there last ffortunes deplore
Lighte doth Shame disclose.
from the Hiest spire of contentmente
my fortune is thy owne.
& ffeare & greefes & paine for my deserts
are my hope since hope is goñ
Harke you shadowes that In darknes dwell
learne to contēne Lighte
Happy happy they that in Hell
ffeeles not the worlds despight.

Ch.Ch.439,ff.3ᵛ,4.

Fond maydes, take warninge while you may

Fond maydes, take warninge while you may
& giue yor selues to amozons play,
Come not Virgines Either
see our Cruell torments wiser
be O be not Coy nor nice
those sinns are ours
for wch in payne we spend our tedious howres,
In gloomy shades wher woe & care
wher solitude & horor are
Dom'd vnto 't by Hells iust frowne,
we now do wander vp & downe.

B.M.Add.MS.10338,ff.34ᵛ-36.

foolish boy forbeare and flee

foolish boy forbeare and flee
henc with thy fond Aertillere
Though I my neck would gladly bowe
and beare thy soft yoake tis not now
as when I first persued the game
my strength and age are not the same
yet I no more of time will spend
when venas Sports are at an end
for he that liues to please A wife
Leads A vaine and fruitelesse life
that part of loue if I might haue
my wish should last bee in the graue :

How should I euer hope to woe
a mistrisse that can nothing doe
you sparkes of loue that yet remaine
rise then and kindle to A flaime
and cupid soone the torch com light
make one blase more and then good night
yet wold she baith mee with her kisses
soft imbraces such sweet blisses
into each uaine fresh flood would bring
and turne old autome into spring
and shee in me new heate inspire
would phenix like growe young in fyer

Drexel MS.4041,ff.38ᵛ,39.

Forbeare fond Swaine I cannot Love

1.   Forbeare fond Swaine I cannot Love
2.   I prithee faire one tell me why
   Thou art not cold *1.* you do but move
   to take away my liberty *2.* Ile keepe thy
   sheep while yᵘ shalt play
   Delight shall make ech month a May
1.   Those pleasant are unthrifty houres
2.   Thou shalt have the choicest flowers
   Wax and hony milke & wooll
   of ripest fruites thy belly full
1.   My flock shall feed by thine *2.* Not so
   but let yᵐ undistinguisht goe
1.   I can afford no more ah cease
2.   Love come so farre may yet encrease
1.   Ech day Ile grant a kisse *2.* Our blisses
   must not conclude but spring from Kisses
1.   Then Shepheard love thy fill *2.* I shall
   who knowes how much loves not att all.
1&2. Then draw both our flockes up hither
   That we may pitch our folds together
   Amidst our chast enjoyments keep ourselves
   as blamelesse as oʳ sheep Our selves. [them selves?]

Fret on fond Cupid, curse thy feeble bow

Fret on fond Cupid, curse thy feeble bow,
and those dull shafts yt are so blunt, so slow,
   I can't bee harm'd,
   my brest is charm'd,
proud Caelia's coynesse whom I woo'd in vaine,
makes mee resolv'd never to love againe.

Let Vulcan whet thy blunted arrowes, love
And steale them wings frō Venus fleetest dove
   vse all thy arte
   to peirce my hearte
When thou hast shot thy quiver empty, then
I'le laugh and bid thee shoot them o're againe.

Lambeth Palace MS.1041,ff.32,32ᵛ.

fye awaye fye what meane you by this

fye awaye fye what meane you by this,
did you not loue me when you did kiss,
wherin could I offend you soe soone,
       O tell me tell me
that you soe roughly tumble me downe,
as if you meant to kill me.

what do you meane thus on me to lye
closeinge my lips wth yors when I crye
was euer man soe falce as thou Art
       O tell me tell me
to kiss when Murder is in thy hart
for now thou meanst to kill me.

doe you not blush me thus to vncloath
methinkes yt syght you rather should loath
Heauen defend me what doe you call
       O tell me tell me
the weapon in yor hand wher wthall
you goe About to kill me.

I feare tis a thinge will breed my shame
mercy shield me are you not to blame
to press a woman yts like to dye
       O tell me tell me
why doe you giue me cause to crye
Ods body man you kill me.

B.M.Loan MS.35,f.7ᵛ.

Gentlie, gently prethee tyme

Gentlie, gently prethee tyme,
doe not make such haste away :
to be hasty is a crime,
then where loue entreats to stay,
Stay stay preithee stay make not such cruell hast,
Least presents brought to[o] late may be disgrac'd

Humbly humbly you poore lines,
kisse ye Virgines gentle hands,
shee in whom soe greate worth shines
such obedience Comands
And tell her though ye yeare be scarce a youth
your masters duty is att perfect growth

Euer euer may true Joie,
in that breast sleep still and sure,
And lett Venus gentle boye
giue noe wound but what hee'll cure
Till as thou Inioy'est and quonquerest all harts
loue, know, and recompence all thy desearts

Ch.Ch.MS.Mus.87,ff.14^v,15.

Gently o Gently wthout fright

Gently o Gently wthout fright,
vnclovd those starrs, most lovely bright
truth thou Father of cleere fame,
give to hir a fairer name,
yen to each possessing sperritts,
yt not knowe hir waies of merritts,
everlasting Joy dwell heere,
rise rise O rise bright eyes,
and make night cleere.

Go & choose w^t sport you will

Go & choose wt sport you will
as yor fancy doth invite
search out pleasures take yor fill
of ech Senses best delight
but let me wn I shall play
sit and kisse my howers away.

Goe & seeke some other love

Goe & seeke some other love,
Mine hath bid thee quite adiu,
Twenty thousand thou maist prooue,
before one that's halfe soe true

Get thee gone, and tell me when
thou hast suffer'd paines like me,
if thou wilt to Hell againe,
and condemn'd a Lover bee.

I am now my selfe & free
like the falcon farr am flowne
and cann pearch on every tree
making day and Night mine owne.

Never shall a captiv'd Hart
more be seated in my brest
I can now repell Loves dart
Drinke good wyne & take my rest

Sooner may lost sighes returne
Then for me to loue againe
sooner may the rivers burne
then ere I will Court my paine

For that hee whose Bonds [Bands?] are lost
and againe In-slav'd will bee
lett him in loves Hell be tost
and there double damn'd for mee

Bod.Lib.MS.Mus.b.1,ff.164ᵛ,165.

Goe bidd the Swañ in Silence dye

Goe bidd the Swañ in Silence dye
& her departinge Songe lay by ;
Or Elce to thee Cheruba come,
to Singe her Epicedium.
that Soe whilst shee doth thy rare voice admire,
shee wth such Musique rauisht may Expire.

Goe empty joyes

Goe empty joyes
wth all your noise
& leave me here alone
In sweet sad silence to bemone
yor fleet & vaine delight
whose danger none can see aright
whilst yor false Splendor dimmes his sight.

Go & insnare
Wth your false ware
Som other easy wight
And cheat him wth your flattring light
Raine on his head a shower
Of hono^r favour welth & power
Then snatch it from him in an hower

Fill his bigg minde
Wth gallant winde
Of insolent applause
Let him not feare all curbing Lawes
Nor king nor people's frowne
But dreame of something like a Crowne
And climbeing to it tumble downe.

Let him appeare
In his bright spheare
Like Cynthia in her pryde
Wth f-----ke [frantike?] troopes on evry side
Such for theire number light
As may at last orewhelme him quite
And blind us both in one dead night

125

Welcome sad night
Greifes sole delight
Your mourning best agrees
Wth Honors funeralls obsequies
In Thetis lapp he lyes
Mantled soft securityes
Whose too much sunshine blinds his eyes

Was he too bold
That needs would hold
Wth curbeing, reines yr day
And make Sol's fiery steeds obey
The sure as rash was I
Whoe wth ambitious wings did fly
In Charles his waine too Loftily.

I fall I fall
whom shall I call
Alas can he be heard
Who now is neither lovd nor feard
You who wont to kisse ye ground
Where ere my honourd steps are found
Come catch me at my last rebound.

How ech admires
Heavens twinckling fires
When from their glorious seats
Theire influence gives life & heate
But oh how few there are
Though danger from yt art be farre
Will stoope & catch a falling starre

Now tis too late
To imitate
Those lights whose pallidnesse
Argues none inward guiltinesse
Theire course is one way bent
The reason is thers no dissent
In Heavens high Court of Parliamt.

Goe thow my soule to thy desired rest

Goe thow my soule to thy desired rest
angells conduct thee where thy trve love lies
there shrowd thy selfe vppon her naked brest :
waite thow one her with loves attentives eyes.

Make her to knowe how deere I doe her love
more then my life for shee is natures Joy
tell her that I will ever constant prove :
how that I breathe her onely trve love lyes

and while shee sleepes Ø tell her still I wake
Sighinge out teares lamentinge for her sake :

doe this my soule and tell to her the truth
How I had rather dye then her offend
Bid her in mercy to behoulde my youth :
and pitty thee come from her dearest freind.
but if she saith shee wyll not favor thee.
fly then my soule retourne no more to me.

Ch.Ch.M S.439,f.12.

128

Goe thy waies and turne no more

Goe thy waies and turne no more,
cruell & vnrelenting,
since this Mute & Desart shore
is more pittifull then thou,
and theise waues their mourmours bough
to beare a part of my lamenting,
but with my hart y^u farr, farr off art gone,
and I poore wretch, alas am left alone.

Go thy waies since y^u wilt goe

Go thy waies since y^u wilt goe
doe not stay to answere no
Like y^ie selfe thy vowes are true
ever changing old for new
Since y^u hast beene false to many
be not constant unto Any.

Yet I will not curse those Eyes
Where thy witching beauty Lyes
Nor desire y^t forme defact
Where so vile a mind is plact
W^th thy beauty few dare strive
W^th thy falsehood none alive.

Live y^u still pride of Citty
Void of Love as voide of pitty
Be not tide to two or three
There is choise enough for thee
And w^n y^u art out of date
Then repent thee all too Late.

To ye woods Ile take my flight
There is harmelesse chast delight
There I neede not hope nor feare
There I will all Love forsweare
And as y^u fledst me before
So Ile fly thee ever more.

Now w^n all thy store is spent
If thy false heart chance relent
Or revert thy foul disdaine
To recall me back againe
Thou shalt heare me thus reply
Oh I dare not lest I dye.

Bod.Lib.MS.Don.c.57,f.38.

God of winds, when thou art growne

God of winds, when thou art growne
breathles and hast spent thy store,
when thy Raging blasts are gone
I Can furnish thee with more
I Can lend thee sighs that ar
fitter for thy Churlish warre.

Flow noe More yee rugged Seas
Nor you swelling watters rise
for your labour I can Ease
from the Ocean of myne Eyes
And your Empty streames suply
though yee Ebb Eternally

I Can lend yee Tempests too
from my wild distracted brest
for Compard vnto my woe
Warrs are peace, and Tumult rest
Noe seas Can greater troubles moue
then a poore Maides shipwrackt loue

B.M.Add.MS.31432,f.31.

Good Susan be as secrett as you can

Good Susan be as secrett as you can,
you knowe your husband is a Jealous man,
though you & I doe meane noe harme nor ill,
yett men take woemen in the worst sence still
And feare of Hornes more greife of hart hath bred,
then wearing hornes [hath caus'd an aking head.]

Great Julius was a Cuckold & may I

Great Julius was a Cuckold & may I
hope to keepe my Sockett dry :
where too consent where shall ye mopish third
thrust out his hand & hatch ye bird
or if he Could were itt not better
for him not to know then to abhor

If he loue not then whers the cursed guilt
not to saue yt, yts as well Spilt
If loue yn oh th‿unsufferable payne
to loue & know he loues in vaine
who euer found ye footsteps of his pride
yt did last lye by her side.

Butt she loues other men him she not scants
then where or what can be his wants
theres nothing missing of yt wonted store
who can who would haue more
he whose vast soule desyres more then all
his desires must Catch a fall :

Drexel MS.4041,ff.64,64ᵛ.

Greife com away and doe not thou refuse

Greife com away and doe not thou refuse,
(as loue hath done) wth me to spend thy dayes;
And if sad stories or distressed newes,
can cause thee staye, I'le finde a thousand wayes
to tell loues Tragedies, & bloodye fray's.
Nor feare thou Ought yt we shall disagree
for None thou hast, nor seeke I any pittye.

Wilt thou but staye & I'le make loue to thee
since thou the faithfulst follower of loue Art
for let loue fayle thou Holdst thy Certaintye
of thee theres none yt may not showe som part
wherfore sad greife Abyde wthin my Hart
Nor feare thou Ought yt we shall disagree
for none thou hast nor seeke I any pittye.

B.M.Loan 35,f.2.

Ha! Posanes, by my loss of peace tis shee!

Ha! Posanes, by my loss of peace tis shee!
Seruljna, the Cruell & ye fayre wee see;
shee whom I soe Ofte haue nam'de in teares!
still her pow're she beares & I my feares!
for I must loue Seruljna,
for I must loue Seruljna!

Judge, Judge O yee Gods, breake I my vow
to dead Licymella, though heere I Bow!
O noe, ye beautye & ye Glory of the playnes,
ye delight & Sadnes of the swaynes,
is devine formde Seruljna,
is devine formde Seruljna.

'Tis she inherrits her Mynde, her forme, her face,
soe full of glorye & Eternall Grace;
theres ye brow y^t will not Frowne,
& ye Eyes that must not Mourne;
for they are Grey-Eyde Seruljnaes,
for they are Grey-Eyde Seruljna's!

see see, those Ruby folds aboue her Chin,
y^t Gaurd those Richer flocks wthin,
O what a pearly, Glossye fleece theye weare,
then Jasons farr more Rich more fayre
for tis whyte Toothde Seruljna,
for tis whyte toothde Seruljna!

stop, stop in loue & beautjes name,
those wand'ringe blushes on yonder playne,
see how they start, & shoot, looke how they Hyde,
i' the shadye Curles of Polydores bryde
ye softe, Browne, hayrde Seruljna,
ye softe browne hayrde Seruljna!

she singes, & playes, O y^t voice, those hands,
loues Chaynes, & Charmes, that all Com̃aunds ;
vnvalewd heere, for whoe from those Eyes can goe,
let Em, & be punishde soe,
shee'le be still Seruljna,
shee'le be still Seruljna.

for all ye Busnes & ye beautye of her Mynde,
is dead Polydore, ye valient & ye kinde ;
that youthe shee lou'de, for witt & vallor famde,
wch wth his faythe, ye Charmer Charmde,
& shee is now his Seruljna,
& shee is now his Seruljna.

That blacke, is One of blest polydores locks,
more prizde by the Nymphe then Al her flocks
bless me, his Gen'ivs from those Hils of Snow wee see,
that Snow y^t melts to none but thee,
for shee's ye Chaste Seruljna,
for shee's ye Chaste Seruljna.

B.M.Loan MS.35,ff.132ᵛ-134ᵛ.

Had I a Trumpet, and that Trumpet Fames

Had I a Trumpet, and that Trumpet Fames;
a sheet of Marble and a pen of steele,
I would proclayme & graue some Noble Names,
soe Loude, & deep, Tyme should not make them feele,
his Sythe or teethe, for they should careles stand,
vntoucht beholdinge his lost Runinge Sande.
   it maye be thought,
   I that haue sought,
soe much ye glory of the smoother Sexe,
maye striue to rayte it now aboue myne Owne;
wch shall be yet vnknowne,
that hope and feare maye Equallye perplex
both vs & them, whose favors I would keep,
till deathes Cold hand leade me to my last sleepe
   The pen I only dip in Inke
   theyr names shall sinke
but tipt wth golde theyr names shall Ryse,
wing'de wth theyre vertues to the skies;
    beware this is noe dreame,
    now Justice is asleepe,
    One holds her Ballance Beame,
    that better watch will keepe,
    for if you loose one graine
    Alowance is in vayne.

B.M.Loan MS.35,ff.121-122.

Had you but herd her sing

Had you but herd her sing,
how her sweete soule was mounted on the wing,
      as if towld Vye
wth the Caelestiall Spheares,
Apollos Delphick Lyre
Could never thus haue set my soule on fyre,
      nor's Harmony
soe bewitcht myne Eares.

The God of loue's growne wise
has found a New way Now for to Surprize
      by Musiques power
and us his Vassalls Make
For wher before hee tooke
Some few with a betraying smyle or looke
      Thus in an hower
Heel Thousand Captiues take

Hange golden sleepe vppon hir Eye-lids faire

Hange golden sleepe vppon hir Eye-lids faire
         & fill the aire
with murmers soft, Lett all the winds be still
         and to her will,
Fancies & dreames be reddy to obey,
shapes bright and goodly sweet as daye,
appear vnto hir fill her hart,
with Loue and Louers Arte
And in hir dreames lett that sweet forme appeare ;
and growe about hir Necke she holds most deare.

Egerton MS.2013,ff.17ᵛ,18.

Hard harted faire, if thou wilt not consent

Hard harted faire, if thou wilt not consent,
alone to place me thyne, in thy proude Eye,
yet let thy grace soe farr at least relent,
y^t I may serue thee as a vottarye.

when I protest was never Holye fiers
halfe soe religious in his vestry Rites
as I wilbe in seruinge thy desires
And keepinge vigill to thy sweet delights

my Hymnes shall raise thy beauty & thy pittye
whylst my morne Mattens Tune but myne owne moane
thy Sacred name shalbe my Eu'nsonge dittye
and all my Orizons shalbe thee Alone!

O I will fast from Eu'ry loue but thee,
And Only pray y^t thou wilt fauor me.

B.M.Loan MS.35, f,4^v, f.17.

HarK HarK how Bellona thunders

HarK HarK how Bellona thunders,
& harKe how Cupid cryes,
his Arrowes are all broKen,
& hee neglected lies
Our Queene of Loue is fledd away,
and Marse doth Tyrannize

Topsey turuey hey downe derry,
'tis warr y^t maKes ye Souldier merry.

DrinKe & drabb & feare noe end,
wee haue three Kingdomes yet to spend.
The Irish harpe is out of tune,
& all our freinds turnd foes,
Ther's noe man Master of his Owne
& thus the World goes.

Topsey turuey hey downe derry,
'tis warr y^t maKes ye Souldier merry.

A few pray for the Kinge
but most wish noe such thinge,
And they that once had ne're a Groate
doe now like Princes singe.
Topsey turuey hey downe derry,
'tis warr y^t maKes ye Souldier merry.

Harke, harke, me thinkes I heer Loue Saye

Harke, harke, me thinkes I heer Loue Saye
the Sullen tymes are Flowne awaye,
& scatterd Louers maye retyre,
to Renovate their Ould desire,
the Angrye God noe More will Fight,
but Sum̃ons vs to new delight

Returne, returne Faire Queene of Loues
wth all thy Nymphs & peacefull doues
Retorne to Albions Isle againe
and take thy place in Charles his wayne ;
For till wee that Conjunction See
this land will never Happy bee.

Then wth the Sun-shine of yor Eyes
the Amaltheian Horne will ryse
the Tramplde Earth shall Teeme againe
wth out ye Labour of ye Swaine ;
And whylst wee all these blessinges haue
Rebellion shall becom yor slaue.

B.M.Loan MS.35,f.171.

Harke how yᵉ Nightingale displayes

Harke how yᵉ Nightingale displayes,
yᵉ latest pleasures of her Throate,
and dyes Content if her poore Noate
might serue but as one step to raise
A Trophy to yoʳ beautyes prayse.

The rose in whose rich Odours lye
the perfumde Treasures of yᵉ yeare
doth blush to death when you Appeer
And Martyr-like towards you doth flye
To weare yoʳ Cheekes fresh Liuorye.

Aurora weepes to see a light
Outvye her Splendor in yoʳ Eye
the Suñes ashamde to walke yᵉ skye,
And th' enuious Moone growne pale for spight
Vowes ne're to Revell but wᵗʰ Night.

The Saucye wynde wᵗʰ Serules [sencles?] care
(Seeminge to feele soft sence of bliss)
steales through yoʳ hayre yoʳ lips to kiss,
soe Riuals mee, whoe now dispayre
to touch yoʳ lip, cheeke, eye, or hayre.

B.M.Loan MS.35f,25ᵛ.

143

Haue I watcht the winters Nyght

Haue I watcht the winters Nyght,
when ye Curphew-Bell hath Runge;
haue I spent my spirrits my Myght,
weake to Me, to you Most stronge,
shall my functions yors be Euer,
loue me Now or loue me Never.

I haue sworne, & you haue heard
Oathes most firme, & sworne to you
yu did list, but not regard
what I vow'de to show me true;
I haue bin yor seruant Euer
loue me now or loue me Never.

if my Service be Neglected
when wth hart & all I serue
let me saye I am rejected
wher I thought I did deserue,
loue I know is but a fevor
Loue me now or loue me Never.

but if Loue dye of the fitt
when yor phisick may recouer
are you not to blame in it
to kill yor patient & yor Louer,
be not cald my breathes bereaver
Help me now, or cure me Never.

He that would catch and catching hold

He that would catch and catching hold,
that fleeting Aire a womans fauor,
must change like hir from heat to cold
shift Proceaus like all shapes to ha[u]nt hir,
somtime laughing, singing, playing,
next day weeping, sighing praying,
that for all hir witt and skill,
she may be vncertaine still,
wch was earnest wch was Gest
or wch humore likt hir best.

Heau'n & beautye are aly'de

Heau'n & beautye are aly'de,
both are wth like wonder spyde,
both seru'de alike too, & ye waye,
to posess both, is to praye
Coarse Atempts are heere denyde,
but such Courtship as the bryde,
Makes to her thoughts when she would faine,
call to mynde her louers vaine
are heer Admitted, if you trye,
Rougher wayes to win her bye?
Each Motion from yor Mistres face,
is Execution & not grace.

B.M.Loan MS.35,f.74v.

Heauen sinc thou art the only place of rest

Heauen sinc thou art the only place of rest,
and restles man can finde no other peace,
then in those thoughts that are to thee addrest,
lett tempests of all worldly pasions cease
Ø lett frayle flesh noe longer force my mynde
to seeke for rest, where shee noe rest can finde.

Fitzwilliam MS.52D,f.112.

Helpe O helpe kinde Abraham & send

Treble : Helpe O helpe kinde Abraham & send
   for pitty sake to me y^t bosome friend
Bass : Call not bold wretch this chill poore soule from rest
   Eternall Angells warme him in my breast
T : Ah! Tophets melting furnace is my seate
   wing him wth windes to fann my burning sweate
B : Rich man your purple & fine Linnin may
   The unconsuming lakes blacke flames allay
T : No not ye mantled mountaines can *B* : Nor I
T : Send Lazarus all arm'd wth wings y^n *B* : Why?
T : To coole mine all over sulphur'd tongue I crave
   but wth one dropp *B* : One dropp y^u must not have
T : Not a full dropp I crave O lett him come
B : No Dives no y^u gavest him not a crumbe
T : My dogg his sores lickt lett my tongue in lew
   but lick his finger dipt in freezing dew
B : Your wholesome eates may best embalme ye same
T : Alas theire surfett did me thus inflame
B : Thy greife is thus past cure away *T* : How so
B : See ye vast gulfe partes us from thee below
T : Then let him charme wth these still Lowder cryes
   my brethren from dead sleeping Lullabyes
B : Let y^m heare Moses thundring threatnings all
   wth ye neere slumbring watchmans dreadfull call
T : They'le heare one from ye dead first *B* : Can beleife
   or trust be in ye grave? No nor reliefe
T & B : So soone as Lifes small, twined thred undoes
   All fine spun pleasures end in endlesse woes

Hence childish Boy too long haue I

Hence childish Boy too long haue I
mistooke thee for a Deity
    I find too late
thy infant power cannot bribe
      nor yet prescribe
      a role to fate
but what in its vaste wombe is sowne
      must fall on Earth
nor need it Midwife saue its owne
      to give it birth,

Stay e're you fly me and behold
this tree bespangled all with gold
      how bright how fine
this Cedar showes now y^t the Sun
      hath fully run
      to th'noontide line,
But ere this guilded Sun shall fade
      and hast to sett
marke by degrees how fowle a shade,
      it will beget

Lovely cruell : let this tree
not rise in judgment against thee
      for knowe tis true
y^t next dayes noontide doubtlesse may
      this tree repay
      but filch from y^u
Then least too many noones shovld flocke
      e're y^u approve
take warning by this sencelesse stocke
      & y^u will love.

Bod.Lib.MS.Mus.b.1,ff.120^v,121.

Hence flattring hopes. Cease longing and giue Ore

Hence flattring hopes. Cease longing and giue Ore,
It is decreed
that he whome you shall see noe more,
must to beguile your wishes bleede,
O may his faults for euer silent passe,
Since tis his doome,
then which a heauier never was,
to finde his mariage bed his tombe.

B.M.Add.MS.31432,f.43.

Hence vaine delights beegone, tempte mee noe more

Hence vaine delights beegone, tempte mee noe more,
my sorrowes tell mee nowe they must prevaile,
since faith is fledd, ye smiles I did adore
are turn'd to frownes & sadness doth asaile
why shold I then a beautie soe admire
that sends forth nothing from her poizning eyes
but scornes why should I languish in desire,
to tast her sweetes when shee to heaven flyes,
to tell ye gods on earth shee cannot rest
being soe persude wth sighes from one distres't.

Fitzwilliam MS.52.d, ff. 114ᵛ-115.

Here lyes Charles yᵉ first yᵉ Great

Here lyes Charles yᵉ first yᵉ Great
The valiant though vnfortunate
yᵉ Just, yᵉ vertuous pious Prince,
the guiltye for his Innosence
the fayth's defender, Kingdom's Charter,
yᵉ Churches glorye, peoples Martyr.
This men & Angells all doe singe,
the honest man, the Righteous Kinge.

Edinburgh University Library MS.Dc.1.69. 54.

Heres a Jolly couple O the Jolly Jolly couple

Heres a Jolly couple O the Jolly Jolly couple
the spring and the Winter are maried
the rose and the hauthorne so croabed and so Supple
to the bonifier of loue are miscaried.
   they rost they frye
   there flames rise hie
let vs sing let vs dance about them
hold hand in hand a round
such a payre are not found
The world cannot stand without them.

O the pritty tulip O the pritty pritty tulip
So fresh to be lookte on and gaudy
She is to the stomacke as cooling as a Julip
she deserues a fitt warmth is not baudy
   short peace long rest
   bee in there nest
let vs sing let vs dance about them
hold hand in hand a round
such a payre are not found
the world cannot stand without them.

Drexel MS.4041,ff.85,85ᵛ.

Heares non but onelie I

Heares non but onelie I
non heere can vs esspye
then come to thy love
ô come ô come ô come

Ch.Ch.MS.439,f.20.

Hold Cruell Love oh hold I yeild

Hold Cruell Love oh hold I yeild
wthold thy mortall dart
this is a chamber not a feild
nor place to strike a Heart

so oft hast y^u my bosome hitt
so oft destroy'd my parke
y^t all ye heart y^t there is left
scarce makes another marke.

Nay not a teare but y^u hast hitt
Nor any vow or signe
Of sorrow, no delightfull fitt
But y^u hast slaine cause mine.

Or if I needs must dy, for now
I see thee aime againe
Vse thine owne weapons (Coward thou)
And borrow not my braine

Hould ling^ell hould the Coblers silken Twyne

Hould ling^ell hould the Coblers silken Twyne
Oh it is stronge allthough it be not fyne
thrust in thyne Aule and drinke good beere and wyne
vntill yⁱ nose wth Ruby Colour shine
   Advance the Can
   then tall yoeman
   domingo domingo
   hey trolylo trolilo
   hey tro lolylo lolylo
   domingo domingo.

Ch.Ch.MS.439,ff.37ᵛ,38.

How Cruels Loue when shees too kinde

How Cruels Loue when shees too kinde,
it melts the Flesh and Racks the mynde,
it Swels our veines wth hott desires,
and Smoothers vs in our Owne Fyres!
thers noe such Torment to ye Mynde,
as too Much Loue or too Longe Kinde.

O let me Change the Ayre a whyle
you kill me now if you but Smyle
the Sweets wch once I begd from thee
but One drop more would poyson me,
thy Cupids now like Serpents flye
& where they byte my passions dye.

Then Farwell Celia for I fynde
Inconstant thoughts refresh ye Mynde
he that will alwayes Am'rous bee
must practice loues vbiquitye
the wyser know loue cañot dye
whylst nourishd wth Inconstancye.

B.M.Loan MS.35,f.154^v.

How happj' art thou & I

How happj' art thou & I,
that nere knew how to loue
ther's noe such blessinge heer beneathe
what ere ther is aboue,
tis Libertye that Eurj wyse man Loues!

Out Out vppon those Eyes
that thinke to Murder me
And hees an Ass beleiues her faire
whoe is not kinde & free!
thers noethinge sweet to Man but Libertye.

I'le tye my hart to none
nor yet confine myne Eyes
but I will playe my game soe well
Ile never want a prize
tis Libertye that makes me now thus wyse.

B.M.Loan MS.35,f.154.

How long false hope, wilt thou mislead myne eyes

How long false hope, wilt thou mislead myne eyes,
to make me gaze & dye through fond desire,
I must no longer listne to thy lyes,
thou art ye fuell setts my hart on fier.
delude mee not my deare is chast' and fayre,
alas, what comfort doe I thereby finde,
I breath out sighes, shee backe returnes dispayre
to shewe the rigor of a Cruell mynd,
what though hir rosey Cheeke & Amber breath
yeald sweete content to mee it is not soe,
they are ordain'd as messengers of death
to Terrifie my soule where ere I goe,
O no, hir virtue will not lett her kill,
where onc shee Conqueres there shee favoures still.

Fitzwilliam MS.52.D, ff.113ᵛ,114.

How Sad's a Scorch'd Louers Fate

How Sad's a Scorch'd Louers Fate,
     y^t must Create
Fresh Joyes each Minuite to his soule,
     or elce 'twill Rowle
into dispaire, & never more
     renew its Score ;
whylst myne not Cherrishde by the Eye,
     must feare to dye,
nor can Excess of heate, or Cold,
     make it Grow Ould.
then learne to be platonicke and wth mee,
Seeke not to plucke the Fruite, but loue ye tree.

B.M.Loan MS.35,f.177.

160

How should I praise theise sug'red plenties

How should I praise theise sug'red plenties,
y^t deck this Royall table,
or sing theise sweeter feamall dainties
that grace it, would I were able
might I but skipp,
from lipp to lipp
my Rellish should then adoare-you,
or elce descend,
to loves best end,
but neither of both are for y^u,
then doe I love no grapes to[o] high,
soe sayes ye Fox, & soe sing I, soe sing I.

How wretched is he borne or taught

How wretched is he borne or taught
to keepe ye freedome of his will
who armes his tongue against his thought
to speak all good & thinke all ill
whose passions more yn Tyrants are
whose mouth doth only sound of death
whose soul is taken wth ye snare
laid by false fam'd & Comon Breath.

How wretched is ye state wee all are in

How wretched is ye state wee all are in,
y^t sleepe secure in vnrepented sine
when not ye greatest king one earth can say,
y^t hee shall liue to see ye breake of day,
nor saints in heauen, nor blessed Angels know,
whether ye last & dreadfull trump shall blowe
to Judgment of ye liuinge & ye dead
before theise wordes I speake are vttered,
o wake, o watch, o weepe, repent & pray,
o haue in mynd ye last & bitter day.

Fitzwilliam MS.52D,f.111.

Hymen hath together tyed

Hymen hath together tyed
ye lusty bridegroome & ye willinge bride,
& vnto ye Gods they pray
to bannish hence ye longe & tedious day
singe we then & so invite
ye louers freind the still & shadie night
While we touch the tremblinge stringes,
to ad more feathers to her sable wings
Hast then gentle night for wee
know thou hast rites as well as hee.

B.M.Add.MS.10338,ff.39ᵛ-41ᵛ.

I am a lover yet was never loved

I am a lover yet was never loved :
well have I lovd and will though hated ever
Troubles I passe, yet never any moved :
sighes have I geven & yet she heard me never
I would complaine & shee would never heere me
and fly frō love but it is ever neere mee.
Ø hivion [oblivion] onely blamelesse doth bee sett me
for that remembreth never to forgett me.

ffor every ill one semblante I doe beare Still.
to day not sadd nor yesterday contented.
To looke behind or goe before I feare Still :
all things to such alike I have consented.
I am besides my Selfe like him that daunceth.
and moves his feett att every sound that chanceth.
and soe all like a Sencles foole disdaines mee.
but this is nothinge to the greefe that paines me.

Ch.Ch.M S.439,f.15.

I am a poore & harmless mayde

I am a poore & harmless mayde,
And some are pleas'd to call mee fayre,
Noe Ambush yet was Euer Layde,
to Catch mee but I broKe the Snare.
And some ther bee that terme mee coy
'cause in my freedom's all my Joy.

I cannot call my mistress fayre

I cannot call my mistress fayre
allthough shee doth exceede,
wthhold her loue by praisinge her,
o noe, ther's no such neede,
to loue her well wth little show,
is best for praise I see,
'twill make her loue her selfe the moe,
& care ye less for mee,
if praises wold not make her proud,
then wold I singe her praises loude.

Yet must I praise and hope the best,
my hopes and feares soe striues,
tis doubtfull which, yet hope prevailes,
good husbands makes good wiues
then thus resolue an iron hand to beare;
nor smile nor frowne,
but if shee sleepe I'le raise her vpp,
if proude I'le take her downe,
for womans humors they are such,
they either want or haue to[o] muche.

Fitzwilliam MS.52D, f.109.

167

I doe confess I love thee

I doe confess I love thee,
though thou wouldst requite wth scorne,
blest I am if thou vndoo-me
yt of heavenly powers art borne,
life I'le give thee, yet I know
that I gaue, I still should owe.

When the blessed powers shall call
and complaine thy being heere
thinke but of my wofull fall
that of all thinges held thee deare
yeild me but this poore releife
I am paid for all my greife.

I doe confesse that thou art faire

I doe confesse that thou art faire,
But I doe thinke thou canst not loue,
Nor trickling teares nor frequent prayer,
shall from my brest that thought remove

Canst thou keepe back the Tydes swift motion,
Blow out ye Starr-light with thy breath,
Hinder ye Sunn-beames from the Ocean,
Or sing away ye paines of Death

Fetter the swallo[w]s as they fly,
Qui[c]klye banish the heate in fire,
The liquid streames make hott & dry,
And in mankind destroy desire,

Comand the Poles salute with Kisses,
Pinn up ye Orbs for turneing round,
Make me beleive y^t Langor bliss is,
That musick is in thunders sound.

When thou hast done all this then I will bee
content to thinke thou maist loue, but not mee.

Bod.Lib.MS.Mus.b.1,ff.165ᵛ,166.

I envy no mans rest

I envy no mans rest,
but hould them blest,
that sleepe while mine Eyes weepe
& while my hart opprest doth keepe
true time vnto my greife
sans mention of releife,
Sweet sorrow I protest,
thou art vnto my Hart
the ever wellcom guest.

Bod.Lib.MS.Mus.b.1,f.29.

I Gather where I hope to gain

I Gather where I hope to gain
I know swift time doth flie
Those fading būds me thinkes are vain
to morrow that may die
The higher Phoebūs goes on high
the lower is his fall
būt length of dayes gives me more light
freedom to know my thrall
Then why doe ye think I lose my time
becaūse I do not marry
vain fantasies makes not my prim
nor can make me miscarry.

I hold as faith

I hold as faith
what Romes church saith
wheare the king is head
the flocke is mislead
wheare the altar is drest
the people is blest
he is but an asse
which shuns the mass
whearfor I pray
that Rome maye swaye

what Englands church allow
my Conscience disallowes
the Church can haue noe sham
which holds the pope supream
with seruice scarce diuine
with table bread and wine
who the comunion flyes
is Catholicke and wise
that England flowrish best
shall nere bee my request

I know y^t my redeemer liues & I

I know y^t my redeemer liues & I
shall see him cloathed wth iṁortality
& in the latter day shall stand
w^n all things are subdu'd to his coṁand
& though this body crawling wormes devoure
in theire darke empire yet in y^t same houre
w^n trumpets shall rouse me from slumbring night
these very eyes shall see his glorious light
Then fear not deaths shady grotto tis ye way
to y^t faire dawne of lifes eternall day.

I looKd vpon my true loues eye

I looKd vpon my true loues eye
looK'd smil'd & spaKe thus loueinglye
LiKe to y^r eys Or liKe to mine
Our hartes in Motion may Combine
If yt eye moue this moues as oft
to ye same point wth the same thought
if one eye stand they both are fix't
In single Contemplation mixt,
Soe shall our hearts one Joy pertaKe
& with y^r greife my heart shall aKe.

I lost my Heart ye other day

I lost my Heart ye other day
and cannot hope to owne it more
for though she ravisht it away
and since hath beat it ovt of doore,
Yet there it hovering still will bee
what ere vngentle weathers flee,
and sweares oh sweares nere to returne to me,

Yet I have sent both sighs and teares
though neither yet could ever gaine
on this hard hart or win her eare
to render either entertaine
but there her suppliant still it lyes
a sad and scorned sacrifize
and me (alas) for ever more denyes,

Fond heart what dost thou meane to doe
canst thou gaine any grace alone
shouldst thou this folly still pursue,
I must in vaine for evermore
ah then at last perswaided be
els death shall right me vppon thee,
then doe thy worst love hir in spite of mee

Bod.Lib.MS.Mus.b.1.ff.125ᵛ,126,126ᵛ.

I loue but dare not show it for why

I loue but dare not show it for why
I am become all Jealousy
oft times I striue for to recall
my heart & sweare I hate you all,
& this I doe because I find,
my mistris is to others kind
for this loue is noe loue I see
it speaks to all as well as mee

if shee let fall a word from whence,
I may conceaue or doubte sence
then am I troubled in my mind
untill the truth thereof I find
and wth my critizisme show
my Jealous thoughts would all things know
for generall loue no loue can bee
it speaks to all as well as mee

who loues mee must loue mee alone,
& loue mee first Ile second none
that heart that comes not to mee free
shall nere share mine whosoere it bee
Dissembling loue like men of state,
it flatters them whom it doth hate
for that loue is noe loue I see
it speakes to all & takes not mee.

Ch.Ch.M S.1022,ff.22ᵛ,23.

I loue thee for thy ficklenes

I loue thee for thy ficklenes
& great Inconstancye,
for hadst thou bin A Constant lass
then thou hadst ne're lou'de me.

I loue thee for thy wantones
& for thy drolerye
for if thou hadst not lou'de to sport
then thou hadst ne're lou'de me

I loue thee for thy vglynes
& for thy foolerye
for if thou hadst bin fayre or wyse
then thou hadst ne're lou'de me

I loue thee for thy pouertye
& for thy want of coyne
for if thou hadst bin worth a groat
then thou hadst nere bin myne.

Then let me haue thy hart a whyle
& thou shalt haue my money
Ile part wth all ye wealth I haue
t'enjoye a lass soe boñye.

B.M.Loan MS.35,f.89ᵛ.

I must Complayne she doth enioye my loue

I must Complayne she doth enioye my loue
she is to fayre to rich in bewtious parte
thence is my greefe for nature whyle she stroue
wth all her graces and devinest arte.
to forme her to to bewtyfull of hew
shee had no leasure left to make her true.

Thus my complaints from her vntruth arise :
accusinge her & nature both in one :
ffor bewty staynd is but a false dysguise :
a Comon wonder that is quickly gon :
And false faire soules cannot wth all their feature :
wth out a true harte make a true faire Creature :

whatt need't thou playne, iff thou be still reiectted
the fayrest creature sumtime may prooue strange
continuall playntes will make the still reieckted
if that her wanton mind be giuen to range
and nothing bettere fitts a mans true partes
then wth dissdayne t'encounter ther false hartes.

Ch.Ch.MS.439,ff.34ᵛ,35, and again at 31ᵛ, 32. (3rd verse only here).

I never laie me downe to rest

I never laie me downe to rest
but my deerest love I see
and laughing then she doth me feede
wth what shee waking keepes from me.
Walkinge waking alasse shee doth me pine
lett me but sleepe and all is myne.

I prithee Sweet to me be kind

I prithee Sweet to me be kind
delight not so in scorning
I sue for Love oh let me find
some pleasure 'midst my mourning
wt though to thee I vassall be
Let me my right inheritt
Send back ye heart I gave to thee
since thine it cañot merritt
So shall I to ye world declare
How good how sweet how faire you are.

I Rise, & greiue

I Rise, & greiue,
I walke & se my sorrow,
I Eate, I liue
perchaunce not till to Morrow
I laye me downe to rest & then againe
I Rise, I walke I feede & lye in paine.
Mend thou my state,
ô Joue, I thee Implore,
or End by fate
what thou hast made before.

if I but close
ye couers of my syght
then slumbringe woes
wth dreames my sleepes Affright
And if Awake I seeke to Ease my Mynde
Som new bred cares My troubled thoughtes doe finde
Mend thou my state,
ô Joue, I thee Implore,
or End by fate
what thou hast made before.

or if it be
thy will I should Endure
what vnto me
is Almost past recure
giue me but strength to vndergoe these paines
wch like A torent Runs through all my veines
or mend my state
wch as my daies doe fade
or End by fate
what thou before hast made.

B.M.Loan MS.35,f.1.

I sweare to thee I will begone

I sweare to thee I will begone
    that sweete voyce & looke,
    hath quite vndone mee,
I am in hast Lett me alone,
    to teare out that hooke,
    thus baited by thee,
    But I am caught I feare,
    And shall pay very deare,
for the folly of my prying eyes,
    The more I striue 'gainst fate,
    I fall (alasse) too late
by the search of Curiosityes,

For standing Close behind this dore
    and Ravish't wth Joy,
    by a pleasing sound
Then lookeing in as hearetofore
    ye vnLucky boy
    gave mee this same wound,
    Heareing but halfe could doe
    I must bee peepeing too
And am Scorcht wth Light[n]ing from her Eye,
    for Pitty Close her sight;
    and stopp my heareing quite
Or make vs a perfect Geminj.

I who erst while ye worlds sweet aire did draw

I who erst while ye worlds sweet aire did draw
grac't by ye fairest yt ere mortall saw
now closely pen'd in walls of ruthlesse stone
Consume my dayes my nights & all alone.

Each morning ere ye day Spring did appeare
Wth nat'rall Musick birds did charme mine eare
But now instead of those melodious Straines
Haue ratling fetters bolts & gyves & chaines.

Yf all that love and man hath sworne

Yf all that love and man hath sworne,
were in a womās bosom borne,
she would be deliver'd of
an abhortive or a scoff,
in his heat trust not his troth,
for his vow is not an oath,
in his heat trust not his troth,
for his Vow is not an Oath.

Yf I in woemen would take my delight

Yf I in woemen would take my delight,
yf I in laughter could spend day & night
Live like ye Epicure, in height of Pleasure,
Or like the Miser glutt my sovle wth treasure,
Yf I with Painting and disembling light,
could gloze with Man, and play ye Paracite,
Or if I would with scorne deride ye Poore,
to make theire Miseryes increase ye more,
or take into me Murder, Incest, Rape,
and be beloved for theise vile Deeds and scape,
what covld theise availe me, since needs I must,
loose Glory, Pleasure, Pride, and turne to dust,
nor will theise losses my accompts make eaven,
I'me throwne from God, Eternity and Heaven.

If I seeke t'enjoy yᵉ fruit of my paine

If I seeke t'enjoy yᵉ fruit of my paine
shee carles denyes me wᵗʰ Endless disdaine
    yet soe much I loue her
that noething can either remoue me or mooue her

'Tis not Loue, but fate, whose doome I abyde
you How'rs and you plannets that destiny guide
    change yoʳ opposition
It fits heau'nly powres to be mylde of condition,

you only can Alter her scorne & her pryde
whoe me now disdaineth
    for weomen will yeild
when yᵉ right plannet reigneth.

Yf pleasures where not wastinge

Yf pleasures where not wastinge
they would bee lothed for lastinge
the blussinge Rose queene of flowers
liueth but a few of howres
yett that sweetnes hath satietie
if not quickned wth varietie
Therfore wisely vse yor pleasure
     Age wasteth
     care blasteth
     yor faire treasure
     and when it goes
     it goes in post
     none can boste
     of longe lastinge
     faire faces
     winged graces
     from vs heastinge.

Tenbury Wells MS.1018,f.48 ; 1019, f.3ᵛ.

If y^t I for thy sweet sake

If yt I for thy sweet sake,
should my selfe thy Vassall make,
& at length disdayned bee,
as vnworthy to love yee.
In faith it shall not trouble mee much,
for my hart it shall not tuch.

But I hope I never shall
into such great danger fall,
As to serve wthout respect,
& for love to have neglect.
sure I thinke I am too wise,
to bee Caught with smyling Eyes.

But if yu wilt love, say soe,
or if not, yn Answer noe,
for delights do dangers breed
& wth idle hopes doe feed,
him yt loves & doth not know,
whither shee doth love or noe.

If thou lov'st? ile love againe,
Or if not, I can disdayne,
If yu hat'st, or dost mee loath,
I can Answer yee in both,
Be it so, bee't nere so strange,
I'le doe soe, if yow doe Change.

B.M.Add.MS.11608,f.4.

If thou dost Loue me as thou sayst

If thou dost Loue me as thou sayst,
then doe what I desire ;
that Loue is Sickly and doth waste,
wch yeilds not Equall Fyre :
Tis but a Languishinge delight,
that does in Kisses dye !
Com let vs Triumphe in ye Height,
of all that's thou & I.

What ? shall ye Tyrrant Conscience Aw ?
or Goblin Honor Feare
let vs be one an Others Law
noe sprite but ours appeere.
our loue has zeale Enough to make
religion of our Owne.
and thyne eies light Enough to shake
the Other diuell home

Then in the pryde of all our Joye
Lets fixe Elizium heer
the Only Hell is to be coye
And only shame to Feare ;
Our harts for Conscience shall not breake
nor Fames from Honor goe
All is Religion that wee speake
And Honor that wee doe.

B.M.Loan MS.35,f.155.

If thou doest not loue sacke

If thou doest not loue sacke,
& drinke whilst thou canst see,
thou hast a wretched narrow soule
& I much pitty thee:

Sacke makes the old man young
and nimble for delight
It makes the myser melt his baggs
& makes the Coward fight.

Would'st thou faine be a prince
& scorne the Common rout
why sacke once made a tinker King
therefore thou needst not doubt

Sacke is the purest blood
that runns through bacchus ueines
& he that thinkes of other food
is company for swaines

It is the muses milke
& wise Apollos fyer
theres not a doe ba'kt witt i'th world
but sacke will him Inspire

Then fill A weightty boule
may he neare sorrow lacke
that will not pledge King Charles his health
In pure Cannary sacke?

Drexel MS.4041,ff.48ᵛ,49.

190

If thou dost Loue

If thou dost Loue
   mee I Loue againe.
If my greife moue
   I loue my paine.
but one Kisse giue mee
   I Kissinge dye.
and If thou leaue mee
   Adeiu say I.
ffor Loue my breast doth fill
   wth such a fyer,
as what soe E're you will
   is my desyer.

If thy Mrs be too coy

If thy Mrs be too coy
bid her adieu adieu
& streight goe seeke another joy
for women are like flying shadowes vaine
follow & they'l fly they'le fly
but fly & they'l follow thee as fast againe.

If you a wrinkle on the Sea haue seene

If you a wrinkle on the Sea haue seene,
Ambitious Rise till it A waue hath bin,
And Markt that waue ascending high,
daish downe againe, and in an Instant dye,
Giue into death, begining to a New
till wrapt within themselues, we loose their Veiw,
Soe in Loues Growth, a spark begetts a flame,
and yt burnt Out returnes to Aish againe,
These the degrees and Ends of louers blisse,
from smale to Great, then Nothing is.

B.M.Add.MS.31432,f.10ᵛ.

if you can finde a Hart sweet loue to kill

if you can finde a Hart sweet loue to kill,
yet graunt me this to Reade my latest will;
may all thinges smyle on you, may nothinge cross,
yor wish or will, whoe Euer beare the loss.

May fortunes wheele be Euer in yor Hand
y^t you may Never sue? but still Comaund,
and to these blessings may yor beautye still
be fresh, & powrfull both to saue & kill.

If you will Love know such to be

If you will Love know such to be
ye Lawes of Cupids Monarchy
        yt to refuse
        is to abuse
loves government & I declare
yt such Loves Rebells not his subjects are.

To love is not to be yor owne
Love studies to please ym alone
        Whom it affects
        Wthout respects,
If ought bends & Love confind,
Is but by usurpation Love defind.

If you did Love as well as I
you nothing could or would deny
        But would conceive
        That you receive
Wt you bestow, If this were true
Your heart would Live in me as mine in you.

Imbre lachrymarum Largo

Imbre lachrymarum Largo,
     Genas spargo
Quavis Aurora, Devs cito
     tu venjto,
nunc nunc sine Mora,
     Ora!
Hoc non valet Semper Oro,
     semper ploro,
Cor deficit dolendo; Te te Amo
     Ad te clamo,
Date finem flendo,
     Endo;
Pecatorum Primus Ego
     Hoc non nego
fateor vero sed tu devs,
     Esto mevs
In te solum Spero
     ero
vox pergrata satis
     satis,
Iam Cedam fatis mortuvs,
viuam tamen Hic cum morior,
     caelo orior
magnum, magnum hoc solamen
     amen!

B.M.Loan MS.35, f.139. "An Eccho".

In an arboure of green may

In an arboure of green may
cupid & his mother laye
venus on her sonne did smyle
Cupid sported hime the while
at last hee saide those wanton smyles
mars & all the gods beguiles

Tenbury Wells MS.1018,f.47ᵛ.

In guilty night & hid in false disguise

Tenor : In guilty night & hid in false disguise
           forsaken Saule to Endor comes & cryes
           woman arise call powerfull arts together
           & raise y^t soule wch I shall name up hither

Treble : Why shouldst y^u wish me dye forbeare my sone
           dost y^u not know w^t cruell Saule hath done
           how he hath killd how he hath murthred all
           All y^t were wise or could on spirritts call

Tenor : Woman be bold doe but ye thing I wish
           no hurt from Saule shall come to thee for this.

Treble : Whome shall I raise or call
           Ile make him heare *Tenor* : Old Samuell
           Lett only him appeare

Treble : Alas *Tenor* : w^t dost y^u feare

Treble : Nought else but thee
           for y^u art Saule & hast beguiled me

Tenor : Peace & goe on w^t seest y^u Lett me know

Treble : I see ye Gods ascending from below

Tenor : whoes y^t y^t comes *Treble* : An Old man mantled ore

Tenor : Oh y^t is he Lett me his ghost adore

Bass   : Why hast y^u robd me of my rest to see
           y^t wch I hate this wicked world & thee

Tenor : Oh I am sore distressed vexed sore
           God hath me left & answers me no more
           distres't wth wars & inward terrors too
           for pitty sake tell me w^t I shall doe

Bass   : Art y^u forlorne of God & com'st to me
           w^t can I tell thee y^n but misery
           Thy kingdomes gone into y^{ie} Neighbours race
           Thy host shall fall wth sword before thy face
           To morrow y^u till y^n farewell & breath
           y^u & thy soñe shall be wth me beneath.

Chorus

All Three

: Art y^u forlorne of God & com'st to me

w^t can I tell thee y^n but misery

Thy kingdome's gone into y^ie neighbours race

thy host shall fall wth sword before y^ie face

Tomorrow y^u till y^n farewell till y^n farewell & breath

y^u & thy soñe shall be wth me beneath

thou & thy soñes shall be wth me beneath.

In loue with you I all things elce doe hate

In loue with you I all things elce doe hate,
I hate ye sun that shewes me not your face,
I hate my stares yt make my fault my fate
Not hauinge you I hate both tyme & place.
I hate Opinion for hir nice respects,
the cheifest hinderer of my deare delight,
I hate Occasion for his lame defects
I hate that Daye worse then the blackest Night,
whose Progresse ends & brings me not to you,
I hate the Night because hir sable winges
aydes not my loue but hides you from my veiwe,
I hate my life and hate all other thinges,
And Death I hate & yett I knowe not why,
But that because you liue I would not dye.

Egerton MS.2013,ff.61ᵛ,62 (rev).

In sorrowes drown'd I wast my weary dayes

In sorrowes drown'd I wast my weary dayes
I find myselfe beewrapt wth Clogges of care,
my fickle state vncertaine still decayes,
I lead a life that seemes to mee full rare,
my Joys are fled, my pastymes gone and worne,
my life bewrapt & I my selfe forlorne.

My sugred sweet hath lost his wontd tast
and bitter paine hath lodg'd itselfe in place
my forgon life now yealds me thrall at last
to hide ye shame of fortunes frowning face
my barke of bliss wch wont to floate at ease
now yealds it self a wreake vnto the seas.

not losse of frends hath Caus'd mee to bewayle
not losse of wealth hath Caus'd mee to Complaine
not losse of life or lymes should make mee quayle
but losse of that wch I doe now obtaine
therfor leaue of[f] my trobled thoughts to tosse
noe recompence can Countervaile my losse.

Fitzwilliam MS.52D,f.97.

In the Subtraction of my yeares

In the Subtraction of my yeares,
   I sayd with Tears;
Ah nowe I to the shades below
   must naked goe;
Cutt of[f] by death, before my tyme;
& like a flower cropt in my prime.

Lord in thy Temple I noe more,
   shall thee adore,
No longer wth Mankind conuerse,
   In my cold Hearse
My Age is past ear it be spent;
remoued like a sheppards Tent.

My fraile life like a weauers thred,
   my sinnes haue shred.
My vitall powers Diseases waste
   with greedy hast:
Euen from the Eueninge to the daye
I languish & consume awaye.

And from the dawninge to the Night,
death waights to close my failinge sight.

Egerton MS.2013,ff.49ᵛ,50.

Intice not me with thy alluringe Eye

Intice not me with thy alluringe Eye
to fruitles Loue, alas it is to[o] late;
I am like frozen winter, colde & Drye,
vnapte for dalliance, and Loues deare debate.
Then on some thriuinge plant extend those Rayes,
whose liuely sap may bringe forth tymely fruite,
by those warme gleames, wch on a tree Decayes,
yeilds little comfort to the branche or Roote.
Although the powerfull motiue of thy looke,
is of more vertue than Medeas charme,
yet when delight hath once a man forsooke,
Noe loue or death can doe him good or harme.

Egerton MS. 2013,ff.54ᵛ,55, and again ff. 63ᵛ,64.

Intrudinge hopes what make you heere

Joye : Intrudinge hopes what make you heere:
       who doth not knowe where dead is feare
       yt hope noe longer liveth
       Hope is but physicke in Annoye
       and these are dayes of health & Joye
       all humours now are quiett.

hope : Mistakinge Joy if that weare soe:
       then die must hee that kills his foe
       for soe good reason giveth
       If I be midwife to the sadd:
       I serve noe lesse vnto the gladd
       as best dish of there dyett.

Ch.Ch.MS.439,f.14ᵛ. "A Dialogue of hope and joye".

It tis hir voice, deare m^{is}, sweetest hart

It tis hir voice, deare m^{is}, sweetest hart,
my Little pritty Jug Jug Jug wher art,
from that waitch tower with thorny pikes bespred,
descend to mee on this soft flowre wrought bed.
And let a Thousand loue songs fill myne Eares
with sharpes and flatts of stranger Joyes then feares,
The Primrose, peagle Cowslip, Violett
with heads Just Nodding to keepe tyme are mett.
This tunefull streame shall beare a part with thee,
Or Groane forth deepe sigh'd grounds of woes for mee,
who feare thou'lt leaue me, and noe more by Singing
Breath Airie Soules in Mortalls Euer Springing.

B.M.Add.MS.31432,ff.16ᵛ,17.

John yor my husbandes'man you knowe

John yor my husbandes'man you knowe
why shoulde you vse your mistris soe
you make me breathles heer's good geare
what if yor master now were heere
but good John leave of & be gon
for yet yor an honest man John.

God's bee deere what doe you goe about
what womans able to hould oute
you put me to my shifts soe faste
That longe I feare I cannot laste
but now be quiet & be gon
for yet you are an honest man John.

Will you not leave alas I ffainte :
this is enoughe to vndoe a Sainte :
yor m^r comes for shame awaye :
what should I doe what should I saye :
aye me my breath & all is gonn :
& now yor noe honest man John.

Ch.Ch.MS.439,ff.8ᵛ,9.

Know Lady y^t my Life depends

Know Lady y^t my Life depends
upon your Love & wth it ends
if you can y^n so cruell prove
to one y^t does so dearely Love
you & your vertue Lett me dye
ye example of your cruelty
But w^n y^t I am dead & gone
vouchsafe but you to Looke upon
ye weeping stone sorrowes true signe
& y^n remember it was mine.

Ladyes, you y^t seeme soe nice

Ladyes, you y^t seeme soe nice,
& as Cold in show as Ice,
& perhaps haue held out thrice,
doe not thinke but in a trice,
one or Other may intice
And at last by some device,
set yor Honors at a price.

you whose smooth & daintye skin
rosye lips, or cheekes, or chin
all y^t gaze vppon you wiñ
yet insult not sparkes w^thin
slowlye burne, ere flames begin
And presumption still hath bin
held a most Notorious siñ.

B.M.Loan MS.35, f.61.

Languish and dispaire my hart

Languish and dispaire my hart
& lett thy groanes to Hills assend,
whose force makes wood's to beare a part,
and eyeless ecco pitty lend,
or if those hard harted are,
then vnto Death fly for releife,
and in the dark goe seeke out care,
whose woes may make thee Houle and dye with greife

Last night my fayre resolu'd to goe

Last night my fayre resolu'd to goe,
I wished a day as faire as she
foorth sprange a morne clad all in Snow
as whyte a day as whyte may bee.
proud Snow how durst thou thus compare,
bee thou more white, She is more fayre.

Lambeth Palace MS.1041,ff.30-30ᵛ.

Laugh not fond foole cause I a face

Laugh not fond foole cause I a face
admired through a vaile,
thy Mtris through hir nasty case
did wound thee with hir taile,

such diffirence is betweene our flame,
as reasons diffirent be for thine
must hide herselfe for shame
as mine for modesty.

Mine farr outsparkles p⌒etious stones
through cleerenes of her blood
thine's like the light of old fish bones
or that of rotten wood

Mine's beavty shedds incircled rayes
like glory 'bout hir head
Thine's like Circean Duskish maze
wch witches vse to tread

Mine's like ye dawne of Balmy morne
breake through each little chinke
Thine looks at best like pollisht horne
And just so doe they stinke.

Mine's pearly teares wch none can prize
like falling starrs are shed
But from thy Mistris nose and eyes
Fall drops like melted lead.

Mine's hony-dewy sweats are farre
More sweet then Rose in pride
Thine's like to Sulphur mixt wth tarre
Are issued through hir hide

My Mistris breath exceeds in smell
The sweetest breath of Cowe
And thine in breath doth farr excell
The Carrion rooting sowe

My Mistris leggs the propps of Love
Are cast with purest skyn
Thine's like two Malt sacks ioyn'd above
And vnder buckling in.

Yet thine and mine may best compare
As cheeife in theire degree
For mine exceeds in all y^{ts} faire
thine in Deformety.

Then vaile thine too, for sight_e yt bee
too glorious or too dire
Do's strike with wunder equally
through feare and through desire.

Leaue Leaue to weepe Ornone, & now, moue

Hirrus   : Leaue Leaue to weepe Ornone, & now, moue,
              thy forward foot, to meet a second Loue,
              Laron is dead, to all the world   *O* : But see but see
              whilst I can weep he is not dead to me

Pyrrhon : Dry vp those tears Ornone such sweet Raine
              my deer Ornone should not fall in vaine

Hirrus   : wher Greef steals by, wee giue
              them Leaue to pass ; more Loūers Liue

Ornone : none such as Laron [Lacon ?] was as bloominge beans
              sweet was his Breath his hayre . . . . .

Pyrrhon &
Hirrus   : see how yᵉ Rest is spoken in a teare,
              it profitts not to weep, *H* : nor doo yᵉ dead
              Regard yᵉ tears yᵗ heer on Earth are shed,
              Loue is forgott below *P* : Men layed i' th Earth
              take notice nether of our Greef or merth

Chorus : death would be sweet if those yᵗ Loued heare,
              would Loue Continew, when they once are there ;

Ornone : I gaue him Ribbands & I Made him trim,
              wᵗʰ maiden strewings ; when I Buryed him,
              Ouer his graue I hung my garlands too,
              & wept for him as maids may weepe for you,
              too turfs of grass sweet as a new mowne meade,
              I laid in's graue, for to vpreare his head,
              are these forgott, *P* : as they had neuer bin

Hirrus   : then looke Ornone on yᵉ tree yᵗs Green
              look vpon Perrhon who is young & still
              growes into talles Like a daffadill.
              Loue him Ornone *O* : shall I Loue *H* : loue *P* : O
                    Loue
              & like Laron I will faithfull proue.

Chorus : Joyne hands & Joyne two harts as Loyall
         as men may see
         mongst harts to be
         when tyme hath made ye tryall.

Little Loue serues my turne

Little Loue serues my turne,
tis soe inflameinge
Rather then I will burne,
I will leaue gameinge,
For when I think vppon't,
O tis too paynfull,
cause Ladyes haue a trick
to be disdaynfull

Beauty shall court it selfe,
tis not worth speakeinge
Ile noe more Am'rous pangs,
noe more hart breakinge
those that nere felt ye smart,
let them goe trye it,
I haue redeemd my hart
now I defye it.

Noe More, noe More,
I must giue Ore,
for beauty is soe sweet, it,
makes me pyne,
distracts my Mynde,
& surfet when I see 't.

Forgiue me Loue
if I remoue,
into Some Other Sphaere;
wher I may keep,
a Flock of sheep,
& know noe Other Care.

B.M.Loan MS.35,f.171ᵛ.

Love & I of late did parte

Love & I of late did parte
but ye Boy my peace envyeinge
Like a Parthian threwe his dart
backward and did wound me flyeing :
what remaines but only dyeinge ?

She whome then I thought vpon,
(My remembrance beautifyeing)
Stayes with mee, though I bee gone,
Gone, and at her mercie lyeing :
what remaines but onlie dyeinge ?

B.M.Add.MS.11608,f.69.

Loue chill'd wth cold & missing in ye skyes

Loue chill'd wth cold & missing in ye skyes
ye other suñe flew to my M^{rs} eyes
to warme him but their over ardent light
scorcht his gay wings & him bereft of sight
thence he shrinks downe to shroud him in her breast
but ye cold frost there bred him more unrest
quench't his brand struck him numbe through ev'ry part
& sure had killd him had he reacht her heart
But soone he left her & was heard to say
oh whither shall I now for shelter fly
wⁿ ye faire beame wch I a seat suppos'd
so so it is all of fire & Ice compos'd

Bod.Lib.MS.Don.c.57, f.61.

Love growne proude would governe me

Love growne proude would governe me,
to wch I would not agree,
for small reason I could finde
love should rule a settled minde,
love but glories in fond loveing,
I must Joye in not removeinge,
love but glories in fond loveing,
I must Joye in not remooving.

Loue I obey shoot home thy dart

Loue I obey shoot home thy dart,
tis for a bleeding, wounded hart
whome oft I haue herd to Murmur Tones,
for mee would moue the Ruthles stones.

Fly, fly, why stayes my tardy sence
to quench that flaming Influence
which elce to sinders streight will burne
all wertue in One sacred Vrne

Virgin more soft then Vestall fire
that shootes into vs chast desire
Canst thou forgiue a Savadge beast
that Sacrifizes now his brest

Why dost thou Inly looke and sigh
as if it breathd forth had thy life
O Tyrant loue, for see the Redd
is turned to Palenes, bewtyes dead

May I forsaken be of all
Vnpityed fynde noe funerall
My Aishes through the world be blowne
for loue is dead, and bewtyes gone

B.M.Add.MS.31432,f.38ᵛ.

Love is the Sunne it selfe from whence

Love is the Sunne it selfe from whence
proceeds a quick'ning influence
betweene the Soules of sev'red friends:
        but ye fond vowes
        that it bestowes
        to expresse
        seriousnes,
are but ye Shadowes that it lends:

Should I make them a guidinge Clue
To passe my Censure vpon you,
Then might I from a womans smile
        Judge Love & trie,
        her Constancie,
        or her feares
        from her Teares,
All things invented to beguile.

Give me a Love that is vnknowne
to needles large Expression;
Long shades a setting Sun descrie,
        But when wee see
        They shortned bee
        And are growne
        Small or none
The Sun then & our Loves are high.

B.M.Add.MS.11608,f.64.

Loue throwes more dangerous darts yⁿ death I spy

Loue throwes more dangerous darts yⁿ death I spy
who by experience now Know both there wounds
death peirc't me through yet could not make me dye
loue wᶜʰ A thought me in effect confounds
Death wᵗʰ more mercy kills yⁿ Loue doth mend
Deaths end breeds rest Loue never rests to end
Death doth inlarge but loue imprisons still
Deaths forct by fate Loue willingly doth Kill

Love thy bright Monarchy I now defy

Love thy bright Monarchy I now defy,
since I thy favarite could never be I
will conspire 'gainst all avthority
& find new lights for Independency,
though vertue Beavty Honor all shovld meete
to make my female tyrant faire and sweet
I must forget all these for interest
they are false lights to me if not lik't best

Lucinda wink or vaile those eyes

Lucinda wink or vaile those eyes,
where thousand loues in ambush lyes,
where darts are pointed with such skill
They're sure to hurt, if not to kill,
let pitty mooue thee To seeme blind
lest seeing thou destroy mankind.

Lucinda shut those lipps for feare
The treasures if thy teeth appeare
For Pearles and Corrall men so loue
That for them they all Theeues would prooue
Then shut those lipps & close those eyes
Lest thou conniue at robberies

Lucinda shut that swelling Breast
Least that the Phoenix change her nest
Yet do not; for when shee expires
Her heat may light in thee soft fyers
Of Loue and pitty so that I
By this one way may thee enjoy

Lambeth Palace M.S.1041,ff.31,31ᵛ.

Maidens rise & come away

Maidens rise & come away
Aurora blushes at your stay
The Birds out of their Bushes peepe
to see if you are rose from Sleepe,
Your Louers languish at your stay,
Torment yem not with longe delay,
[let them lead you to the Bowre]
Or Sitt and Kisse you by ye howre,
Or if you'd loose your Maidenheads,
The fields are sweeter than yr Bedds
Therfore Maidens rise I say,
The sheapherds call you Come away.

Marke well this stone, it hydes a precious tresure

Marke well this stone, it hydes a precious tresure,
a pearle, wherin both Heau'n & earth tooke plesure
whoe whylom weded was & brought foorth twins,
God easd her byrth, death freed her from all sines.
Modest in cheere, yet sweetly cheerfull still,
giuing content to all, to none their fill.
Ten yeeres a wife to one she deere did loue,
none Equally to him, saue God Aboue.
her Husband greeues, but all in vaine to miss,
her whom the saincts receaue to joye & bliss.

B.M.Loan MS.35,f.4ᵛ.

Milla the glorie of whose bewteous rayes

Milla the glorie of whose bewteous rayes,
gayn'de heau'ne her wounder and the earthes best praise,
whom Thirsis mette, was faire, & louely to[o],
he lik'te her well, but knew not how to wooe.

They arme in arme into the garden walked,
Where all the day shee endles riddles talked :
Her speech and actions wisely had an ende,
Yet wist hee not where to they did intende.

Shee greeues to see his youth noe better taught,
To gather hime a posie hee her besought,
With that her light greene gowne she then vp tucked,
And Maie for him, and Time for her shee plucked

Which when shee brought he tooke her by the middle
Hee kist her ofte, but could not reade her riddle :
A : foole quoth shee, with that burst out in laughter,
Blusht, ran away, and scorn'de him euer after.

Drexel MS.4175.xvii.

Miserere my maker

Miserere my maker,
O haue mercy on me wretch strongly distressed,
cast down wth sinn oppressed
mightily vext to the soules bitter anguish
euen to the death I languish
yett lett it please thee to heare my ceaseles crying :
miserere miserere miserere, I am dying.

miserere my Sauiour
I Alass am for my sinnes fearefully greeued
& cannott be releeued :
but by thy death wch thou didst suffer for me
wherfore I adore thee
& do beseech thee to heare my ceaseles crying
miserere miserere miserere I am dying.

holy spiritt miserere
Comfort my distressed soule greeu'd for youths folly
purge, cleanse, & make it holy
wth thy sweet due, of grace & peace inspire me
holy I desire thee
& strengthen me now, in this my ceaseles Crying
miserere miserere miserere I am dying.

Turpyn's Lute Book MS,ff.12ᵛ-13.

Musick in time

Musick in time
is without Crime,
musick in place
hath his spetiall grace
musick murdereth maloncoly
other som it bringes to foley
And others to be holy
not so good but maye be Abused
And not so ill but maye be excused.

Filmer MSS.All.d,f.143.

Must I in my most Hopefull yeares

Must I in my most Hopefull yeares,
      at once refraine
her worldes of sweets y^t worldes of teares
      I shed to gaine :
Ah me those joyes, whose wondrous powr's
      vs soe deceaue
y^t yeares seeme dayes, & dayes seeme Howres,
      how can we leaue.

Those Eyes wheron all Others Might
      wth wonder gaze
Those cheekes wherof all peñes may wryte
      A booke in praise
that Syren voice y^t might vllisses
      Eares deceaue
those browes whoe see's, those lips who kisses
      cañot leaue.

wch waye then may I bid Adew
      vnto my deare
in whose farwels delay's I veiw
      & welcomes heere
whose kisses whyle they one forsake
      they me receaue
O straunge y^t lips wee made to take
      both loue & leaue.

B.M.Loan MS.35,f.11.

Must we be devyded now

Must we be devyded now,
in ye springe of all or Joyes
ere the Oxe hath felt ye Plow,
or ye Larke hath strayned her voice?
       sweet then a whyle
       lye still and smyle,
and in thyne Armes enfolde me
       whye shouldst thou feare
       when none can heer
nor anye Eye behold thee.

but my deere I will not staye
nimble tyme I see dos hast
Ile but kiss thee, and awaye
Joyinge in those Joyes are past
       thus as I goe
       begins my woe,
Eury Howre Augmentinge
       till I Obtaine
       those sweets againe
the Mapp of all Contentinge.

B.M.Loan MS.35,f.83.

My hart is fled from mee yet liue I doe

My hart is fled from mee yet liue I doe,
but to maintaine my life must needs haue one
thou thē yt in thy brest dost harbour two,
thine owne & myne yt vnto thee is gonn;
shalt still both courteouse accounted bee,
& cruell if yu send'st not one to mee.

Yet send not backe againe my rebell hart:
our wonted peace cann never bee restor'de,
but let it rest wth thee & neuer parte;
since more then mee hath lou'd thee & ador'de:
deere send mee thine, vnless yu do'st desire,
wth death to end my woes & quench loues fire

Fitzwilliam MS.52D,f.113.

My life is now a burthen growne

My life is now a burthen growne
Oppressd with constant anguish
while sick of greifes I dare not owne
I thus vnpittied languish
but though I burne with secret fires
a heart that is a breakinge,
must needes reueale its fond desires
without the help of speakinge

Then turne O turne those Charminge Eyes
vpon y^r gaspinge Louer
the fatall wound of which he dyes
you quickly will discouer.
But silently to beare his woe
Shall bee your Martyrs glory,
If by one pittying look you show
You vnderstand his story.

B.M.Add.MS.29396,f.109.

My loues as vertuous as yours is when you sware affection

My loues as vertuous as yours is when you sware affection
for so Inflamd religion you keepe in subiection
I cannot tempt you to giue me respect
tis not ye crime but ye man you reiect
       with words so zealous
this same trifle called honor is a pretty witty Couer
to conceale a Louer.

What need a battrye be when as ye fort is resigneing
you will not stopp youre eares att youre one seruants repining
where we affect we doe neuer mistrust
if you would spell loue & Chance to write Lust
       No Interlining
Take a lady in ye humor when the loue fitts vpon her
shele neere thinke of honor.

Drexel MS.4041,ff.57-8.

My Love to shew her cold desire

My Love to shew her cold desire
hath clad her selfe in freeze attire
whiles my Loves passion all on fire
melts wth her beames yt I admire
She by this habit prooves she needs
no helpe externall from her weeds
And yt she Phoebus rayes exceeds
dimm'd wth ye covering cloud he breeds.

My m^{rs} Loves noe woodcokes

My mrs Loves noe woodcokes
yet loves to picke the bones
my mrs loues noe Juells
yet loves the pretious Stones
my mrs loues noe huntinge
yet loues to heere the horne
my mrs Loues noe tables
yet loues to See men Lorne
my mistris loves noe wrastlinge
yet loues to take a ffall
my mrs loues not Some thinges
& yet she loveth all
my mrs loues a spender
yet Loves she not a waster
my mrs loves noe Cuckolde
and yet shee loues my master.

My sweet love is faire to see

My sweet love is faire to see,
and most pleasant to behold
O so beawtiefūll is shee,
that with tongūe can not be told
No it passes all the wits alive,
my Loves beawtie to descrive

O so pleasant and perfect,
O the pearle without compare
O my love my hearts delight
and the comfort of my care
when I was opprest wt pain and greife,
my sweet love was my releif

My love is faithfull and kind
Whose love will never decay
My love cannot chang his mind
Whom he loves he loves for ay
she is endued wt gifts divine
that no love is like to mine

My love is no earthly wight,
My love is the king of glory,
My love is yt lord of might,
that to life did me restore
When I was condemned to lasting pain
my love bought me free again

Lord whom should I love but thee
that loved me befor I knew
When I was thine enemy
sūch great love thou to me show
that spaird not to die thy self
to save me from death and hell

236

Therefor Lord I heartyly pray
that I may love the[e] aright
Lett no vain hope me bewray,
which is wrought by sathane slight
Let me be ever inclined to love
the[e] with my heart and mind

To love things that is here beneath
all is but vain and vanity
but to lock on christ by faith
to that soul more Joy Joy to be
Then all the delights this world untill
though thou hadst y^m at thy will

Now my soul take no ofence
Through the absence of thy dear
trust and hope w^t patience
for that hapy day draws near
O y^t happy day when shall thou see
thy sweet love y^t died fore the[e].

Squyer MS.490,48,49.

My wandringe Thoughts haue Travelde Rounde

My wandringe Thoughts haue Travelde Rounde,
this Little world of womans Ground;
and ther haue seene, as much as Arte
Or Nature can to them Impart.

Vppon the Appinines of Loue
where Snowye Beauties only moue
and in the valleys I haue bin
wth Nymphs whoe Tempt ye Gods to Sin

Through Loues Sweet Ocean I haue Saylde
and all th'inchantinge Syrens hailde
wher Sea borne Venus I haue met
intangled in her Vulcans Net.

what dwels aboue I doe not know
but sure ther's noethinge heer below
that's sweet, or fayre, or good or kinde
but Cloris to Amintors mynde.

B.M.Loan MS.35,f.147.

Noe Falce, noe Faithles Lindamor

Noe Falce, noe Faithles Lindamor,
thy Giddy change Excuse noe More,
the Marriner that Once hath strayde
Through Rocks in watrye Ambush Layde,
shall trust ye Lurkinge Crags agen
e're I haue Euer Faith For men;
My Saked hart in Embers lyes
to thee A Smoakinge Sacrifice;
if thou vppon ye Ruine tread
how should it be Inhabited:
true Loue, Like ye pomgranade swels
wth Rubies bigg in Golden shels,
of w^ch, if one from Other stretch
noe art can Euer heale ye breach;
till by ye Lauish passage Freed
away ye precious Jewels bleed.

B.M.Loan MS.35,f.158.

No fflattring pellow pon my beed

No fflattring pellow pon my beed :
vpon ye ffattall mos and willow,
I lay my much tormented head,
    and sight and weep
    untell I keepe
Just passes with my sorrow :
Thus hardly Can so sad a man
distinguish night from morrow :

My Day is Clouded and my nights,
in misty discontented shrouded
and left quitt loss [lost?] to all delight
    saue but my Crime,
    I hould with time,
no reckning Booke nor Tally,
The ffountains keepes the teares I weepe,
My graue lies in the vally.

B.M.Add.MS.10337,ff.2ᵛ-3.

Noe more of teares I have not left in store

Noe more of teares I have not left in store
to quench my flame, but make it scorch the more
my sighs wch shovld have cool'd my hott desire
blowe my flame high and set me all on fire
noe remedye to coole mee? yes there's one,
if thou wilt gird me in thy froazen zone
there I may turne as thou art, or make thee,
melt thy white snowe, and turne to fire like mee

Noe, noe I never was in loue

Noe, noe I never was in loue,
nor Euer hope to be,
I haue an Art protects my hart
from that fond Lunacye!
And yet I know yt I haue Seene
a world of takeinge faces
& spent much Tyme in fyndinge Out
their sev'rall hydden graces.

This Ladye for her prettye shape
I Often haue Admyrde
that for her fancye & her witt
I sometymes haue desyrde
but yet I never was in Loue.
nor Euer hope to be
vnless some stronger Influence
doe draw my hart to thee.

Noe, she ne're lou'de, 'twas the excess

Noe, she ne're lou'de, 'twas the excess
of myne supposd such happines;
soe when the bagg of gall O'reflowes,
and his faint Tincture outward throwes,
through stayned Opticks (cheated) we
thinke all thinges yellow that we see.

I was all loue, and did relye
on it as if 'twould multiplye;
but loue I finde is not that stone
wch turnes all Metals into one;
his flames like fyre to wax and claye
turnes her to stone, melts me awaye.

B.M.Loan MS.35,ff.84ᵛ,85.

Noe, twas her Eyes

Noe, twas her Eyes,
starrs haue noe Influence
            vpon my sence,
nor could me thus disguise,
these at First sight,
as if I had bin Charmde,
            my wits vnarmde,
& lefte me in this plight,

That, though perchance
I now doe walke and Moue
            and talke of loue
tis but as in a trance,
O I am strucke,
and if she cruell grow
            and leaue me soe
I haue the worser Luck.

            and am vndone,
vnles she doe me right,
            as well she Might,
haue kild me wth a Gun!

B.M.Loan MS.35,f.170.

Nothinge one earth remaines to show so right

Nothinge one earth remaines to show so right
the patirne true of my encresinge care
as philomela with her songe by night
whose ruthfull state I thus to myne compare
with carefule watche she percheth in the tree
when creaturs all Into ther nestes do creepe
so frome myn eyes all sweete repose dothe flee
when men are wonte of course to take there sleepe
she with a thorne against her tender brest
I wth the dart of cruell fates vnrest

This gentle bird her yeldinge voyce dothe straine
to wayle the wronges which progne did endure
I haples man vppone this night complaine
that causles doth mee these greefs procure
and when shee doth her tunes so dolfull frame
as well might moue the heavens to none her plight
oh greefe of greefes yett suche as heere the same
rew not her plaints butt therein take delight
likewise my plaintes which bringe from me salt tears
seem plesant notes vnto my mistris ears.

Tenbury Wells MS.1019, f.5ᵛ.

Now I haue found yᵉ reasons why

Now I haue found yᵉ reasons why,
thy love hath bine soe cold to me
I sought allwaies I could to try,
How to adresse my selfe to thee :

My Heart was free & open too,
as the day to thy brighter Eye,
My song soe sweet as it might woo,
Sad Philomell in loue to dye.

But I am fatt short breath'd & ould,
& theise the reasons plainely bee,
Tis wealth I want thy Pride t'vphould,
My Back's too weak to carry thee :

Though thought may heaue vp a desire,
The fewells gone should feed thy fire
Yet pitty me, but know not why,
Soe wee in loue & pitty both shall Dye.

Bod.Lib.MS.Mus.b.1,ff.116ᵛ,167.

Now in the Sad declenshion of thy tyme

Now in the Sad declenshion of thy tyme,
when all the World forsakes and layes thee by
I but vnveile my loue Maskt in the Prime
of thy Transcendent Glories for mine eye
Jugde thee not Woman but a Deitye,
And till those Rosses blushing on thy Cheeke,
Those lyllies and those Violetts were seene
to wither thus Till all those sweets we seeke
in Ruine Lay, I could neare begin
to Court thee without Hazard of a Synne.
Freed from all Riuall doubts and Jealous feares,
by tymes Rude hand Those Reliques I adore
My flames increase although thy Bewty weares
And in this Temprett Season loue thee More
Then in that scorching heate, that went before

B.M.Add.MS.31432,f.8ᵛ.

Now may I see the time hath beene in vaine

Now may I see the time hath beene in vaine
        hey ho hey ho
wch I haue spent in sighs her Love to gaine
        ah heavy hey ho
    & since she will not please
    to cure my disease
        oh pittifull hey ho
    I finde it such a thing
    yt I am forc't to sing
        A Lamentable Hey ho.

Now may I say yt bootlesse were those teares
        hey ho hey ho
Wch for her Love I oft shed in her eares
        Ah heavy hey ho.
    But since she will not deigne
    To ease me of my paine
        Oh pittifull hey ho
    I wounded wth ye sting
    Thus mournefully must sing
        A Lamentable hey ho.

Now though I sing yet doth my heart lament
        Hey ho hey ho
The Labors lost wch in her love I spent
        Ah heavy hey ho
    And since yt I must dy
    For want of her mercy
        Oh pittifull hey ho
    I dy upon Loves string
    And dying now do sing
        A Lamentable hey ho.

Bod.Lib.MS.Don.c.57,f.33.

Observe yᵉ Hellespont a while

Observe yᵉ Hellespont a while
yᵉ Poe yᵉ Thames & fruitfull Nile
how their full streames do swell wᵗʰ pride
& scorne yᵉ bankes through wᶜʰ they glide
till in yᵉ vaster Ocean they all are
tost & found no more
So Mrs other beauties be
but tributes & a part of thee.

Of all the birds that ever I see

Of all the birds that ever I see
the Oüle is the fairest in her degree
For all the day long she sits on a tree
and when the night comes away flees she
Tiwhit, to you Sir
knave this song is weell süng,
I make you a vow,
and he is a knave that drinketh now.
nose, nose, nose, nose,
and who gave you that Jollie red nose,
Cinamon and ginger, pepper and cloues,
made me to have this Jollie red nose.

Squyer MS.490.57.

oft have I searcht both court and towne

oft have I searcht both court and towne
and country village too,
the blacke, the faire, the lovely browne,
bold, coye, and simple too,
yet amongst all I ne're could finde,
one y^{ts} more constant then the winde.

If nobly borne she scornes to bee
confined in her love
If riches make her melt wee see
Variety shee'le prove
And shee whom want betrayes, no lesse
Counts change her only happinesse.

Since all will trye I'le now no more
Court dang'rous constancy
But I'le change object and adore
this sweet variety
For taught by their example, I
love nothing now but Libertye.

Lambeth Palace MS.1041,ff.35ᵛ,36.

O doe not goe from vs and bring

O doe not goe from vs and bring
so sad a winter on the spring,
that but new borne yeilds vp hir flowres,
only to deck those sweeter browes of youres;

but must you needes sleepe there mine eyes
in gloomy shaddowes ne're to rise,
from yr dead Traunce, till the bright Ray
of your eye, rouze you and restore my day,

Hart and eyes both embrace the night
like Batts and blinde Oules who the light
dispise, slomber out th''ours Adjourne our paine,
till wee reivew those saveing Beames againe.

Bod.Lib.MS.Mus.b.1,ff.62ᵛ,63.

Oh doe not melt thyselfe in vaine

Oh doe not melt thyselfe in vaine,
for I can never love againe,
I doe forgiue thee ev'ry Oath
you broke, each protestation too
whereby I'ue gain'd such vitious groath
as I cann frame myselfe to doe
ye same, and be as false as you,

Yet could you pay repentance meete
to palliate ye paines I rue.
I would accept it with as sweet
and faire a way as you could doe
thus greiv'd if I againe shovld sue,
But then (alas), I reason loose,
and then againe you will refuse,

for sure you must
if I love againe begin
repent this sorrow as vniust
since by't I multiply my Sinn
For they're weake lovers who admitt
a renovation of their fitt
since who are wise ne're venture soe,
twice to encounter a knowne woe.

Bod.Lib.MS.Mus.b.1,ff.118ᵛ,119.

253

O Fayre Astrea, whyther, whyther art thou gone

O Fayre Astrea, whyther, whyther art thou gone
thou Art our life, well beinge, peace & Joye;
wthout thee wee are all Confusion,
& Madly shall our selues & Ours distroy
Retorne, retorne, & thy Sad Servants saue,
Elce Bent to Ruine, or at best a graue.
A dawning showes, O welcom Fayre Aspect,
Clowd vs noe More & paeans weele reflect.

B.M.Loan MS.35,ff.169,169ᵛ.

O faire content where do'st thou dwell

O faire content where do'st thou dwell,
in a Rock, or in a Cell,
where thy peace of conscience? tell.
from a wounded Hart I fly
there I would but cannot dye,
in a woma[n']s wonton eye,
never yet content durst lye.

O I am Sick, I am Sick to death, tis soe

O I am Sick, I am Sick to death, tis soe!
I, & tis Fitt ye world should know
as well as I,
wherfore I dye;
from whence? from whence that Flash of Lightninge came,
that turnde my wytherd hart into a Flame;
I Burne! I Burne! Oh how I Burne
yet doe not vnto Ashes turne;
but like a Fyrye statue stand,
Ready to melt at her Com̄aund;
but o, how Cruell is my fate, y^{t} shee,
Burnes not! but should an Icye Mountaine be,
of powre to kindle such Tormentinge Fires,
& her Owne Frozen hart know noe desires;
but yet if fates giue waye,
y^{t} vncontrold I may,
Once Claspe her Snowy Figure in these Armes?
Ile quench my heate, or Thaw those Icye Charmes!

B.M.Loan MS.35,f.151^{v}.

O let mee still and silente lye

O let mee still and silente lye
wthout a sigh a teare or grone
I will not haue her know
yt I doe slight my sorrow soe
for they who morne & sigh & weepe doe try
if they can giue their greife a remidye

may she not Justly mee repay
with scorne for on a front soe high
if I doe seek a cure
& not glorie to indur
hir cruelty who would not shackles lay
one captiues yt would run away

the verye course her pride requires
when thy obedientt hart hath run
& ye dispa[t]ching rage of loue hath don
ye ackte of age thy youth undon'
making thy seacret fiers
consume all fuell but desyers

if this exchange thou not repent
as great a merrack[l]e thou⁀art gron
as shee though she againe should loue
ay me alas but when hir hart of stone
resolues not to relent
die an⁀tt shall bee thy monument.

Drexel MS.4041,ff.12ᵛ,13ᵛ.

O Let sweete slumber dreames

O Let sweete slumber dreames
thy maiden thoughts attend
& ioyes from passions free thee,
O let no tast of ill displease
but love wth Joy assend
yt all may Joy to see thee
O rest in peace & rise wth Joy
sweete loue of night faire queene of day.

The winds sweete musicke makes
To lull thine eyes asleepe
And pleasure striues to grace thee
The rivers flouds & seas are calme
And all thinges silent keepe
In their high worth to place thee
More blest liues none sleepe then in peace
And all true Joyes thy Joy increase.

Darke clouds the skie doth fill
To summon all to rest
And misty fogges and drooping
The fayry Nimphes are now abroad
Wth Musicke sound addrest
To please thee wth their hooping
I must be gon farwell till day
My loue my life my onely Joy.

Ch.Ch.MS.Mus.87,ff.15ᵛ,16.

O loue, are all those Arrowes gone

O loue, are all those Arrowes gone,
which shott Chast fire[s]
or is it my poore fate alone
to feele desires,
whose End doth fright us, to begin,
and makes the thought of loue a Sin.
Break hart, what strang affection will it proue,
That is not lust, if None dares Call it loue.

B.M.Add.MS.31432,f.41.

Ø mortall man how longe wilte thow remaine

Ø mortall man how longe wilte thow remaine
drowned in sinne & daunger for to dye.

Lifte vp thine harte & tourne to christe againe :
with all meekenes & most humilitie.

Oh, Oh, where shall I lament

Oh, Oh, where shall I lament,
or where shall I
my follyes past repent
yt I may dye;
ye burthen of this loathed life,
to me is like a sea of greife;
what then remaines,
to Ease my paines,
only to dye;
and since my smart,
cañot be Easde by Art,
Com gentle death, & wth thy darte
peirce her hart,
yt from this loathsom life would part,
weep weep myne Eyes,
& never Cease to Crye,
till you haue purchasd Ease,
vnto yr Mistres Miseries.

B.M.Loan MS.35,f.12.

O smoother me to death

O smoother me to death,
wth thy sweet Balmye breath,
whyle thy deere mouth Affoords,
whole kisses, & halfe wordes,
And Cruell longe betryinge
the pleasure thus in dyinge;
yt I soe slayne may pardon thee,
and all the world maye Envye thee.

B.M.Loan MS.35,f.43.

Ø That this last farwell

Ø That this last farwell,
coulde from my Lipps more gently part
and weare not such a deadly spell,
as spoaken it must breake my harte

or that the Clue of Loue,
by hir vnkindnes weare soe worne,
as hart frō hart, might hurtles moue
& neither in themselues be torne

But neuer feare hir hart,
in that it hath not wrought soe deepe,
for though to me the word depart,
be death to hir it is but sleepe

The Losse thus only mine,
Lett me att once be rather rente
then Langushinge away to pine,
& wᵗʰ hir Hertique scorne be spent

Then take this Last farwell,
first vnto you & then to Loue
he neede not feare an other Hell,
whoe both yʳ heates att once doth [proue?]

Egerton MS.2013,f.11ᵛ.

On A cleere morne as phoebus run his Race

On A cleere morne as phoebus run his Race,
he chancde to spye my Dorolizus face,
Amazde at such a sublynary starr,
wth dubble speed, he driues his blushinge Carr,
into a Cloude, & there Enragde he lyes
Inventinge how to darken those bright Eyes

Goe phoebus cleere thy face, Collect thy Raies
And from those starrs wch to thee tribute payes
Draw back thy light, then in thy Greatest pryde
view my Loue, a starr, not yet deifyde
And if thou Canst out shyne her, thou shalt bee
Againe Our wonder, & noe longer shee.

On. On Compassion shall neuer Enter heere, tis tyme

On. On Compassion shall neuer Enter heere, tis tyme
to throw away respects and Clyme,
shall Crooked feeble Age
my aspiring thoughts asswage.
Giue me preferment then,
and hang a father thats Threescore and Ten
Tis wrought merily Carowse and quaff, and freely giue
ourselues all liberty yᵗ liue,
respect and duty must
shyne, wher it may Not rust.
Giue me preferment then,
and hang a Father thats Threescore and Ten

B.M.Add.MS.31432,ff.42ᵛ,43.

265

Or you, or I, Nature did wronge!

Or you, or I, Nature did wronge!
you made too faire, & I too true,
Most beautious you Near heard my Songe,
yet was it Euer framde to you,
& I can never turne ye leafe,
though I singe still, & you are deafe.

O be you still ye same you were,
though I would not be what I am,
yor beauties change is my poore care
I doatinge, master of my blame,
for yor fresh coullers will away,
but my true loue shall nere decay.

yor precious blossomes beinge shed
and my etternall loue aliue
I'le say in you beauty is dead
& what it was to prayse I'le striue,
for in yr worth I'le not be dumbe
since of it I must make my tombe.

Orpheus, O Orpheus, gently touch thy Lesbyan lyre

Alecto   : Orpheus, O Orpheus, gently touch thy Lesbyan lyre

Orpheus : My Harpe is out of tune, nor Can my voice,

chaunt one sweet accent, *Alecto* : the whole Stigyan Quire

expects thy Harmony. *Orpheus* : Restore my choice

the faire Euridice for till she Come,

ther wilbe noe blisse in Elizium

Alecto   : Thou hast thy wish, shes heere *Orpheus* : O wher *Alecto* : Behold

her from yt groue of mirtles rissing [*sic*]

Orpheus : Soe day breakes, black night surprizing,

Euridice, *Euridice* : my loue *Orpheus* : let us infold

Euridice : let us infold *Euridice*) :

Orpheus) : each others shadow, *Euridice* : that the Ghosts belowe

Orpheus : that the Ghosts belowe

Euridice : may see our kind Embraces they will grow

Envious of yt our hapines *Alecto* : O Noe.

Euridice : Then will I lay my Cheeke to thyne

and hang vppon thy snowy neck.

Orpheus : Rivers Soe, Or flames intwyne,

that from Severall heads doe break.

Euridice : yet watters when they Joyne are Cold,

and flames materiall soone expire

Alecto   : yours, are Eternall, *Orpheus* : Never Old

cause kindled by a Chast desire

Chorus   : Kisse then kindly and Embrace,

while we in these shade[s] doe dwell,

Nor be weary of the place,

True loue makes a heauen of hell,

True loue makes a heauen of hell a heau'n of Hell.

B.M.Add.MS.31432,ff.39ʳ,40,40ᵛ.

Out of the horror of the deepe

Out of the horror of the deepe,
wheare feare & sorowe neuer sleepe
      to thee my cryes
      in sighs arise
lord from dispaire thy seruant keepe
      O lend a gratious Eare
      & my petitions heare;
ffor yf thou shouldst our sinnes obserue,
and punish us as we deserue,
      Not one of all
      but then must fall,
since all from their obedience swerue
      yet art not thou seuere
      that wee thy name might feare
Thy mercyes our misdeeds transcend
my hopes vppon thy truth depende,
      disconsolate
      on thee I waite,
as weary Centinells attend,
      the chearfull Morn's vprise
      with longe expectinge Eyes.
O you that are of Jacob's race,
in him your hopes and comforts place
      his praises singe;
      the liuinge springe
of mercy and redundant grace;
      for he will Israell
      redeeme from sinne and Hell.

Egerton MS.2013,ff.50ᵛ-51ᵛ.

Pale Inke, thou art not black Enough of hew

Pale Inke, thou art not black Enough of hew,
t[']express a Mournfull sadnes & a true ;
get thee vnto some darke & cruell groue,
there beg of death a sader shape to haue,
for maiest thou com at last wth some beleife,
to be a Seeminge partner in my greife ;
And procure Admittance to my Sorrow ;
wch of nothinge but of death can borrow.

Perfect and endles Circls are

Perfect and endles Circls are,
and such of late myn and my loues heart wear,
    but if now ye red
    be from my poor heart fled
you are ye caus why it is pale and dead
for gazing on your eyes my heart stood still
amazed was, and thus became both pale & ill
Smile now and what before was whit you'l view
carnation beeing restord by you.

Lambeth Palace MS.1041,f.23^v.

Poore Pensiue I O're Chargde wth woe

Poore Pensiue I O're Chargde wth woe,
wth Sad & deep dispayre
oft wish that face I ne're had knowne,
Or that thou wert less faire
but to Compare my Loue wth thyne,
I needs must breath a groane
& wish thy loue were like to Myne,
Or myne like thyne were none.

but hence proceedes this feare of myne
I sighe and know not whye
I would Accuse that hart of thyne
but then my hart must dye!
I liue to sighe, to greiue, & groane
thus doth my cares renew
I haue noe hart, my hart is gone
& stolne awaye to you

Oft doe I wish that thou mayest feele
my pleasure or my paine
but if thy hart be made of steele
send me my hart againe!
thou'lt not deny my hart I know
doe but consider thyne
for thyne noe wound at all can show
the wounded hart is myne.

B.M.Loan MS.35,f.117.

Poore things be those vowes we boast on

Poore things be those vowes we boast on
on w^t cause so ere we ground y^m
how much thought & care they cost one
& yet leave them where we found them
Letters written in ye dust
wch evry breath doth move
are pure steel to womens trust
& live worlds beyond their Love.

Yet I know she is a woman
To whose Love my faith I tye
Ist not strange y^t there is no man
Lesse beleives theire sex y^n I
Yet on[e] told me who had tryd y^m
Of thousands one may constant be
But I doubt me he bely'd them
Through his craft to Couzen me.

Yet enlisting hope doth woe me
To think one woman may be true
And in yor Angells shape comes to me
Oh God w^t power then rests in you
Then if Destiny hath given
More y^n ever I could weene
Ile sweare you only dropt from Heaven
And till now were never seene.

Bod.Lib.MS.Don.c.57,f.39^v.

Pox on pelfe why should we loue it

Pox on pelfe why should we loue it
since theire damned all yt couet
let vs thirst for racie wine
yt creats mortals devine
tis want of sack
should make vs sad
not monies lacke
then boyes drinke
sing & laugh & not thinke
on base chinke
but quaffe
for sacke yt brought vs on
will bring vs off.

Trash will not the mind innoble
nor can durt remoue a trouble
tis the quintesence of grapes
that a sordid soule new shapes
to drinke & sing & laugh & not thinke
on base chinke
but quaffe
for sacke yt brought vs on
will bring vs off.

mor sharpes the wits then studiying
mount youre cups though yee times
seemd to stop & oretop our designes
rich wine will lends a hand to spring new mines
tis want of sack
should make vs sad
not monies lacke
then boyes drinke
sing & laugh & not thinke
on base chinke
but quaffe
for sacke yt brought vs on
will bring vs off.

Drexel MS.4041,f.109.

Pythagoras th'art right

Pythagoras th'art right
now doe I surely finde
ye transmigration of my minde
my soule of wch even now I was possest
keepes mansion in my Caelia's breast
so I[t] quite voide of reason & of sense
mooves only by her influence
Since soules thus meetes you Dyetyes choose whether
give me my soule or bodyes joynd together.

Bod.Lib.MS.Don.c.57,f.18ᵛ.

Rejoyce whyle in thy youth thou Art

Rejoyce whyle in thy youth thou Art,
and wth delight make glad thy hart,
and let not slip one minutes pleasure
for tymes not to be bought wth Treasure ;
Ould age on thee will Creep too fast,
as all thinges to An End doth haste,
in wch Tyme thou wilt Sadly saye
I haue noe pleasure in this daye.
then Cheer thy soule & liue free,
to all delight thy youth leades thee,
but yet Remember the dread daye of doome,
And that for all thou must to Judgment Come.

B.M.Loan MS.35,ff.24ᵛ,25.

Restles streame thy self persuinge

Restles streame thy self persuinge,
And yet from thy self still flyinge,
staye thy Course, and waues renewinge
heer A sorrow like to dyinge,
wch when thou shalt haue knowne,
goe tell the Sea, that all her store,
of bitternes Affordes noe more.

Tell her my Silvia whoe alone
Sole Gaurdian was of all my Joyes
death late hath strooke, & she is gone
whose loss noe wealth can Counterpoise
Eu'n in her beauties prime
And triumphd On that daye, Aboue
the Conqueringe force & powre of loue.

Alass I now can say noe More,
sighes stop the way to this discours
farwell, goe help thy Queen to Roare
I'le giue thee leaue to take thy Course,
but rest not more then I,
And for thy loss of tyme thats past,
My teares suffice t'increase thy Haste.

Rise, rise Princely Shepherd & bee Arbiter

Juno : Rise, rise Princely Shepherd & bee Arbiter
'twixt 3 contendinge Goddesses, quit feare
& freely speake wch choycest beauty shall
for victory enioy this Golden Ball.

Paris : How can a sylly Earthlings wandring Eyes,
dazled wth terrour at yor deities
censure yt beauty wch they dare not veiw.

Juno)
Venus) : Thou mayst, yu must, Jove never speakes vntrue.
Pallas)
Paris)

Juno : I'le make yee Monarch & thy power shall swaye,
all Europe, & the spacious Asia

Pallace : I'le giue yee such transcendent wisdome, as
shall all th'admired learned'st Greekes surpass.

Venus : I'le giue yee Her, her fayrest who alone,
alone on Earth is Beauties Paragon.

Paris : Still most vnfortunate most wreatched I,
markt out for woe, by fate & destiny,
what? shall my vote offend two Goddesses,
& (oh vnaequall) onely one must please.
A Monarchs mighty powre who would despise.

Pallase : Oh, but it is most Godlike to be wise.

Paris : What higher bliss then beauty can bestowe.

Juno : The proudest beauty to a Crowne will bow.

Paris : And wisdomes vnfound depth, who would not sound?

Venus : Beauty the god of wisdome can confound,
not one of all ye Gods, hath scapt yt wound.

Paris : wch of you three, can I ye fayrest call,
but beauties Queene, & shee must haue ye Ball.

Paris
alone &
then all : Beautie's ye soule of humane Excellence,
ye Eyes blest obiect, rapture of ye sence,
Vertue's most glorious Garment, lov's rich shryne,
Earths onely Phoenix, natures worke divine,
ye Common Idoll of All harts, ô then,
beauty yt masters gods must Conquer Men.

Roome make roome you that are fled

Roome make roome you that are fled
downe and sleepe among ye Dead,
looke heere yu Spirritts, yt doe groane,
Heare and pitty this poore Maides moane,
what is this life, a Tale wch tould,
we pass away, wax pale and cold,
Tis but a sigh a print in Sand,
a Tree oft shaken by Deaths hand,
The Soule an Actor is disguisd wth flesh,
& after death a bridgroome greene & fresh.

Sacred Flora Crowne this ffeild

Sacred Flora Crowne this ffeild,
wth the Choice of All devices,
Mirhe and Balsum let it yeild,
fragrant Odours Muske & spices.
let noe Rude vnhollow'd feet
press these Tender flowers,
soe securely may we Meet,
Our desyred Howers.

See that primrose wch my deere
wth her dainty foot did Tread
for her Absence sheds a teare
And wth ruth hangs downe her head,
how that bed of roses lyes
wher we two satt kissinge
as vnwillinge to Arise
whylst they finde her missinge.

Glorious Tytan turne thy rays
or if that must be denyde
send vs many such like dayes
make this Eb A flowinge Tyde :
wher my piñace freely maye
safe at Anchor Rydinge
lye wthin that pleasant Baye
Euer ther Abydinge.

B.M.Loan MS.35,f.20ᵛ.

Saye, must wee part

Saye, must wee part,
Sweet mercies bless vs
both in Campe, & wildernes;
can wee soe farr straye to becom less
Circular then wee are now,
O noe that selfe same Hart, that vow,
y^t made vs one shall nere vndoe,
Or Rauell soe to make vs two.

Say puritan ist come to passe

Say puritan ist come to passe
that thou must heare a play or masse
      which wouldst thou Chuse
truly in such a doubtfull case
itt well becomes the child of grace
      doe as the spirit shall infuse
but hadst thou to thy frydayes dish
a Capon or a dish of fish
      which wouldst thou eate
capon is for ye babs of grace
giue sinfull papist ling or place
      such supersticious meat.
Loe here a puritan Chatholicke aright
who loues his gutt but doeth the spiritt slight;

Say puritan ift be thy hap
to be inioynd the corner capp
      wouldst thou denye
ye I profest babilons whore
this Idol did Erect nay more
      itt sauoures of Antiquitye
but wouldst thou be content to were
the new cap that hides sinne not haire
      sir nam'd Calot
so itt be not of spannish leather made
ueryly⌢it cannot be gaine said
      by any good zelot
Loe here a puritan Chatholicke aright
who loues his gutt but doeth the spiritt slight

Say puritan doest loue a quire
or the holy bellowes which inspire
        the organs sweet
sure no there satans instruments
not fitt for holy Sions tents
        the faithfull hold they be not meate
but wouldst thou not use any guile
to heare a brother preach a mile
        from text or sence
not if he rayle religeously
gainst surplesse & conformitye
        the spirit doeth despence
Loe heare a puritan Chatholicke aright
who loues his gutt but doeth the spiritt slight

Say puritan if glorious paint
in rich church windowes wouldst not faint
        at such a sight
fye fye one painted glasse why there
Idolytre is full as Cleare
        to pure eyes as is the light
But should a painted sister lye
prostrate wouldst thou not cast thine eye
        one such a Ruth
wel may the spirit subiest
to steale a glance or kisse yee the rest
        should be in naked truth
low [loe] here a puritan Catekis'd aright
who loues whores painted elce all paintes doth slite

Drexel MS.4041,ff.118ᵛ-120.

Say sheaphards boy who makes thee greeve soe sore

Say sheaphards boy who makes thee greeve soe sore,
loue is yᵉ Sweet of life then Sigh no more.
yf I were loue I would not vse thee soe,
then banishe fruitles woe,
and take mee Swayne, whose hart thou long hast had
if thou wilt make thee gladd.

Singe wee of loue, o lett our Joyes aspire,
and fill our harts with Chast and holy fier.

Loues burni[n]ge brande is couched in my brest,
ah glad am I to honoure this behest,
and yet his fuery doth inforce my smart,
making a pheonix of my faithfull hart sweete nimph where art.

Singe wee of loue o lett our Joyes aspire,
and fill our harts with chast & holy fire.

Fitzwilliam MS.52D,f.100ᵛ.

See ! see yᵉ bright light shines

See ! see yᵉ bright light shines
& day doth rise
shot from my Mrs Eyes
like beames devine

Her glories doe appeare
& view yᵉ purest light
streames from her sight
wⁿ she shines clearely here

But vaile her lidds ah! yⁿ youl find
how night is hurld
about yᵉ silent world
& we left blind

The darkenesse seemes to prove
for ought we see
tis only she
makes night or day to move

Then smile faire Caelia lest oʳ borrowed light
wⁿ yoʳ suñe setts perish in shades of Night.

Seest thou not nann to day my pretty nanny

Seest thou not nann to day my pretty nanny
my hartͤ delight to day my sweetest hunny
banisht her company I liue in misery
so hatefull is the lyfe of wretched Tommy
kept back from her I loue & neuer shall remoue
Ø hardest hap to proue for my sweet nanny

her face bewitch't my hart, her eyes comͫands me
her grace Angellike, her loue wᵗʰstands me
my penn can wittnes bee how well still I loue thee
yett sighes nor teares by me, can no whitt moue thee
thy hart is hardned soe, to be my deadely foe
Alass I dye for woe, yet still I loue thee

my lute soundͤ dolefully, for thy vnkyndnes
my voyce singͤ mournfully, love sleepes in blindnes
giue light sweet light to me, & lett me shyne by thee
doe not eclipsed bee, by meekenes obiect
but deare thy loue return, so shall I cease to mourn
& bless that I was bourn, to be thy subiect

The heau'ns wᵗʰ teares do weepe, to see my mourning
the wyndes do sigh full deepe, to see thy scorning
the riuers raging glyde, to see thy endles pryde
no creature can abyde, my causles payning
all things to me consent, wayling my great torment
the stares themselues relent, at thy disdayning

Sweet nann come pitty me, ease my tormenting
lett greif released be, imbrace contenting
for what wilt gayne to thee, a tyrant for to bee
to kill the hart of me, thy faythfull Tommy
be not so cruell then, woemen were made for men
lett me fynde favour then, of my sweet nanny

Then shall my penn still wryte, thy loue com̄ending
my lute to thee shall sound, sweet wthout ending
my voyce thy prayse shall sing, the heau'ns leau their weeping
the wyndes shall cease sighing, Pitty sweet nanny
the riuers smothe shall winde, all things shall thee applaud
for that thou hast made glad, the hart of Tommy.

Turpyn's Lute Book MS. Rowe 2, ff.14ᵛ-15.

Seest thou those dyamonds wch she weares

Seest thou those dyamonds wch she weares
on yt rich Carscanet,
& those on her descheveld hayres,
fayre pearles in Order sett:
beleiue younge man, all these were teares
of sundry louers, sent,
in bubles, Hyacinths, & Rue,
all Embling discontente,
wch when not warmed by her veiw,
through Cold neglect each one
Congeald to pearle or stone,
wch now, ye spoyles of loue, vppon her,
she weares as Tytles   ) of her Honor;
                    Trophies)
O then beware fond man & thus surmise,
she yt will weare thy teares; would weare thyne Eyes.

B.M.Loan MS.35,f.27.

288

Sett to the Sun, a diall that doth passe

Sett to the Sun, a diall that doth passe
The Loadstone through a Christall Glasse
You'le see the wandring Needle howe it will
dance East & West but to the Pole stand still.

What wonder then if I vnfixt have gone
by manie beauties yett can chuse but one?
Mine Eyes the Glasse, the Needle is my Soule,
Love is the Loadstone, My beloved the Pole.

B.M.Add.MS.11608,ff.12V,13.

Shall I despaire of my resolv'd intent

Shall I despaire of my resolv'd intent
because my Mrs is of high descent
No that shall spurre me on in my pursuit
& in ye action make me resolute.

Shall I because my Mrs is unkind
Frantick myselfe wth a pplexed minde
No rather will I smile at such like folly
Then so tormt my selfe wth melancholly.

Shall I deject my selfe for Love & dye
Because my Mrs frownes on me not I
Neither her frownes nor yet her high descent
Nor great unkindnesse shall me discontent

For know my Spirritt (Lady) to be such
That if you doe, I can neglect as much
Therefore for ever euermore adieu
You are so coy yt Ile have none of you.

Bod.Lib.MS.Don.c.57, f. 98.

Shall j then weep or shall j sing

Shall j then weep or shall j sing
whilst I Reflect on euerything
and thinke how I haue been the ball
for adverse fate to play wthall
Alass how sadly I Resent
the Loss of all my sweet content
my fickele freinds away they Run
and court naught but the Rissing sun
thus am j left in dismall nighht
beraft of comfort and of sight
No Gentle Eare to hear my moun
approches but am Left aloune

B.M.Add.MS.29396,ff.109ᵛ,110.

She is too Cruell, alas too Cruell

She is too Cruell, alas too Cruell,
like furious flames presumeinge ;
wth sorrow dryde thoughts prepared fuell,
loues pretious fruites Consuminge ;
what Though Sole Empres she of beautye be,
& mirrour of perfection ;
Honour Ecclipsd wth Crueltye
Casheereth fayre protection.

Sheppard in faith tell me

Sheppard in faith tell me
how much dost thow love me
wonder & ioye doth tell
how deere I doe love thee
tell me how much
Ø never such
heavenly faire maides our feilds doe blesse
nor ever will
woe to me vnkind sheperdesse
but ø deere still.

Shepherd saw thou not my fair lovely Philis

Shepherd saw thou not my fair lovely Philis,
walking on yon moūntaine or on yonder plaine;
she is gone this way to Dianas foūntaine,
and hath left me wounded with her high disdaine
Ay she is so fair, and withoūt compare,
sorrow comes to sit with me,
Love is full of feare, love is full of care,
love withoūt this cannot be
    This my passions pains me,
    and my love hath slaine me,
    Gentle shepherd play a part,
    Pray to Cupids mother,
    for I know non other,
    that can ease me of my smart.

Shepherd I have seen thy fair lovely Philis
where her flocks are feeding by the river side
Aah! I much admire she is fair exceding
In surpassing beauty should surpass in pride
But alace! I find they are all unkind
Beauty knows her powrs too well
when they list they love, when they please they move
thus they turn their heaven to hell,
    where theire fair eyes glancing
    like to Cupids dancing
    Kulles well for to deceave us
    with vain hops deluding
    still then praise concluding
    thūs they love thus they leave us.

Thus I do despair love her I shall never
If she be so coy, lost is all my love
but she is so fair, I will love her ever
As my pain is Joy which for her I prove
If I should her love, and she should deney
heavy heart wt me would break
Though against my will tongue thou most be still
for she will not hear the[e] speak

    Then wt kisses move her
    they shall show I love her
    lovly love be thou my guid
    But I'le sore complain me
    she will still disdain me
    beauty is so full of pride.

Squyer MS.490.58,59.

Si aliquis vult esse frater

Si aliquis vult esse frater,
bibat ille ter vel quater,
bibat Seruus et ancilla,
bibat sponte hic & illa,
Bibat Domina & herus
Ad potandum nemo Serus.
    Pro mortuis
    et pro Viuis
    pro Liberis
    et Captiuis
pro Rege et pro Papa
bibatur vinum sine aqua
per plena pocula poculorum   Amen.

Sylly boy wert y^u but wise

Sylly boy wert y^u but wise
y^u hadst no neede of eyes
but wanting y^m as well as witt
how canst y^u finde ye way to hitt
Away you wagg away away away
Leaue of[f] your cunning play
you shall not feele my heart
poore knave he does inquire about
& now his hand hath found it out
Oh there he stickes his dart.

Silly Heart forbeare

Silly Heart forbeare
those are Murdringe Eyes
In whose flames I sweare
Cupid Lurkinge lyes
    see his Quiuer
    see his bow too
    see his Dart
Fly ô fly thou ffoolish Heart

Venus triumphs there
In a simpringe smile
Pritty dimples are
Loues alluringe wiles
    Shun those glances
    Fly her fancyes
    sheild each part
Hast ô hast vnwary Heart

Greedy Eyes take heed
Those are scorchinge beames
Causeinge heartes to bleed
And eyes bring streames
    Loue lyes watchinge
    with his bow, bent
    And his dart
whet to wound both eyes & heart

Thinke & gaze yor fill
Foolish heart & eyes
Since you loue yor ill
And yor good despise
    Cupid's threatninge
    Cupid's dartinge
    And his brand
Mortall power can not wth stande.

Lambeth Palace MS.1041,f. 1^v.

Since gratious Ld if y^u wthold thy hand

Since gratious Ld if y^u wthold thy hand
a little while I can no Longer stand
grant y^t I may for thy helpe still be calling
y^t y^u maist me uphold w^n I am falling
y^u knowest I can not raise my selfe but need
thy aid who workest both ye will & deed
Oh y^n assure me thus much by this token
make mine heart sound & yet Lett itt be broken.

Synce my Joyes thoroughe Phillis frownes

Synce my Joyes thoroughe Phillis frownes
are Extinguisht and throwne downe
Synce my delight is deade in me
thoroughe Phillis Crueltie
I will Laye awaye my weeds of Blewe
and take me to my Tawnye hewe
all the so longe my songe shalbe,
my garlande is the willo tree
willo willo willo willo willo willo
willo willo willo willo willo willo
willo willo willo willo willo willo.

B.M.Add.MS.15117,f.16.

Since thou wilt goe fond hart and I, must Lye

Since thou wilt goe fond hart and I, must Lye
condemnde to shad's till Quicknde by thyne Eye
this sad Advantage thou wilt ad to mee,
to make me Sencles how to worship thee;
for canst thou thinke my sacrifice should sweate,
rich gums vnto thy name depriude of heate
Oh then retorne, and Kindle my desyre,
soe shall thine Alters smoak who ther bringst fyre;
and my congealed brest shall drop to teares,
in witnes of thy Faith, & my vaine Feares.
soe does ye darkned Muscovite bemoane,
th' vnhappy Farwell of his Suñ, & groane
in his cold Frozen shade, in wch he maye
court ye black night alone, & grope for daye
but if he chaunce to spye his buried sun
retorne bright in his resurection
he stops, & startled twixt Joyes and Feares
he to it bowes, & thawes himself to teares.

Since 'tis resolud that I must dy

Since 'tis resolud that I must dy,
O spin not out my Destiny,
But thinke y^t Martyrdome hath paine,
In which each minute I am slaine:
Tis cruelty sublim'd to giue,
No more, then makes mee wretched liue.
Death sent mee in one fatall blow,
A fauour were no overthrow,
So should I fall, to those bright eyes,
At least a pitt'd sacrifice:
And thou surviue only to be
Admired for thy cruelty.

Sing aloud, Harmonious Spheares

Sing aloud, Harmonious Spheares
Let yor concords reach Jove's eares.
Play yor old lessons ore againe,
& keepe time in ev'ry straine
For now ye Gods do listen to yor Lay
As they [are] passing through ye milky way.

Scorch not fire nor freeze thou aire
Whilst yor Deities be there
Hence you clouds & airy Meteors
Fogs & such vnwholesome creatures
Keepe all yor regions pure all passage faire
Now ye blest sp^{ts} wander in the Aire

Sweetly sweetly lovely mirth
Kisse the bosome of the Earth
Make them garlands of the spring
Send for all the birds to sing
The Gods approach I heare theire fluttering sound
And now now now now now they touch ye ground.

Sing sing Syren though thy notes bring death

Sing sing Syren though thy notes bring death
perfume ye Aire wth thy sweet breath
ye winds are still ye river stayes
delighted wth thy pleasant layes.
The Gods doe listen & Love sweares
you drown'd ye Musick of ye Spheares.

You turne cold winter into Spring
And hearing you ye Swañs doe dye [sing?]
The hearts revive wch you have slaine
And wounded Lovers Loose yr paine
Whilst I and Love these wonders speak
The trebles of my heart-strings breake.

Sittinge downe to her repast

Sittinge downe to her repast
Juno like in loftie speare
eyes did wonder how shee gracd
bewties selfe wth bewties cleere,
when shee speakes as non soe well
harts drawes wisdome from her voice
when shee smiles all graces dwell
and in dimpled cheekes reioyce

Humaine sences grow devine
by one vowell of her speeach
ther doth highest wisdome shine
sent to Rule & Rulinge teach
blessed starrs of her alone
desiringe of earthly faire
Blessed Clymate of her throne
& each place of her repaire.

Ch.Ch.MS.439,f.17ᵛ.

Sleepe, close not vp m̄ne Eyes, and if thou doe

Sleepe, close not vp m̄ne Eyes, and if thou doe
present me nothing elce but horrid woe,
that my Ambitious greife may living know
the paines yt sovles doe feele in Hell below,
Com ô thou elder birth, and lett my breath,
suck the grim̄ Image of thy Brother Death.

Sleepe in yor Lidds y^u loved shades

Sleepe in yor Lidds y^u loved shades
of my vaild Sunns, I vow,
tis not to spare my blood y^t thus
I spill my teares on you,
greife and affliction only due
to me are Justly bent,
to give me a wasting life t' indure
a lasting languishment,
that when mine eyes can weepe no more,
my Hart may bleed, and I
because I liv'd a longer life,
a longer death might dye.

Sleepe, sleepe faire virgin, sleepe in peace

Sleepe, sleepe faire virgin, sleepe in peace,
pitty thou dyd'st [dye'st?] wthout increase
strangrs weepe that doe but heare
how good thou wert, and how soone gon,
well may the looser spend a Teare,
that knew the ioye of such a one,
To thy sweet Memory shalbe paide
a plentious deare-one every Morne and eaven,
Farwell for ever, Farwell for ever, lovely Maide
a virgin-lamp on Earth, a starr in Heaven.

Bod.Lib.MS.Mus.b.1,ff.25ᵛ,26.

Sleepe O sleepe thou Sacred dust

Sleepe O sleepe thou Sacred dust
amongst the ashes of ye Just
till a comitte of angells come
to trumpet out thy Martirdume
    ye vrne wch holds
    such sacred moulds
who can suppose should otherwise appeare
then as A pulpet whilst thy dust is there.

Sweetly Sweetly mast thou rest
'mongst the ashes of ye blest
& hugg him gently earth for theres
an earring kinge we are proud to beare
    heauens prouidence
    hath tooke him hence
thus iuelers oft cabinet y^t gemme
which people rather gase at then esteeme

Come o Come yee Seraphins
ioyne all in consort in sweet himnes
spread all youre winges and let each one
Joyne hand in hand to make A throne
    To beare him streight
    To heauens gate
Bring glories many and let each shine Cleare
to conduct y^{or} fellow angell to his spheare.

Drexel 4041,ff.76,76^v.

Sleep, sleep Softe, you Colde clay Cindars yᵗ late clad

Sleep, sleep Softe, you Colde clay Cindars yt late clad
soe faire ye fairst soule ye vaste Earth had;
in thought (Aye me) of you I inlye feele,
A Num Ice (through each faylinge Artyr[i]e) steale
like a deathes sleep, welcom as ease to paines,
water to thirst, freedome to whoe remaines
Haspt in strikt Ir'ns, Heere Heere still let me Mourne,
till I, (like Niobe) to stiffe Marble turne;
or fallinge Melt away in this sad dreame,
(Cyane-like) into a Silver streame.

B.M.Loan MS.35,f.64.

Soe Phebus rose as if hee had last night

Soe Phebus rose as if hee had last night
cald to account ye Moone for all ye light
she ever ow'd, and lookes soe full of scorne
and pride as if twere payd him all this Morne,
Lord of my Heart awake, and wth thy high
smooth numbers, charme this Deity till he
forgetfull of his course, his Chariot stay
and quite depriue th'antipodes of day,
Thou Sun of Honour rise sing now of Love
till thy soft tunes the colder Hermite move,
vntill the sollemne Judge his limnes aduance
to tempt the crooked Matron in a daunce.
Sing Dirges now and sullen obsequye
till fate repent their essence is so high
from passion raisd that they can nere obtaine
the greife wch gentle Poets faine,
Till on the Rockes faire Scythians sit and mourne,
as Virgins doe at some kind Lovers urne,
Till rock's themselves ore-heare't and each to haue
ye showe of greife shall melt into a waue.

Some loue Marce and some loue Venus

Some loue Marce and some loue Venus
but I loue bacchus and selenus
for when I am sad what ere I lacke
I curs my greife wth good old sacke
sack of old they calld it neckter
Achillis dranke ont so did hector
Ageax & Vlisses sly
and all the greeks and soe will I
Then drinke it of & nesters dayes
Thou shalt seruiue and were the bayes.

Drexel MS.4041,ff.95ᵛ-96.

Speake, speake, at last replye

Speake, speake, at last replye,
tell me must I needes dye?
Art merciles, art cruell than,
cruell to kill a man?
a man y^t loues, & loues thee, thy foe
& Enimy to death doe.
Kill not a frend a Guiltles frend,
one y^t never did Offend;
noe not in thought or Conscience,
if loue be noe Offence.

Speake you that heare, now Cloris sings

Speake you that heare, now Cloris sings,
wedding hir cleare voyce to the strings
hir hand awakes; growes not ye wind
dumb? and the checkt aire calme and kinde
that late so rag'd and roar'd : look, look,
doe but obserue yt chiding brooke,
how mute, th'attentiue wel pleas'd waters stay,
that but now muttering ran so fast away
Ah Cloris, can'st thou then create
such sence in thing's Inanimate?
Yes, but alass, while thou dost charme
the Dead, thou dost the liueing harme,
se faire enchauntress se, mine Eyes
and Hart their hurtfull properties
haue gaind, and must, till thou thy charmer vnbinde,
outflow the Rivers, and out sigh the winde.

Bod.Lib.MS.Mus.b.1,ff.94ᵛ,95.

Stand statly Tavie out of the codpis rise

Stand statly Tavie out of the codpis rise
And dig a grave betwene thy M^rs thyges
Swift stand then stab till she replyes
Then gently weepe and after weeping dye
Stand Tavie and gaine thy creditt lost
Or by this hand ile never drawe the[e] but againe a post.

Drexel MS.4257,f.1ᵛ.

Stay ô stay why dost thou fly me

Stay ô stay why dost thou fly me,
turne agayne and lay thee by me
I am neither Snake nor Adder,
Ile not hurt thee come and try me,
None shall of thy sight be gladder,

Com and rest thee on my Bosom,
Ile but braide thy locks and loose em,
Dew and drench them with the showreing,
of mine eyes that hither woos em
with a fraquent streame downe powreing

Yet not drowne nor hurt them sweetest
if for feare of that thou fleetest
theyle be dry if thou but eye them
or if thou shalt think it meetest
with my sighs Ile fann and dry them

See loue I have made thee posies
pictures of thee Pinkes and roses
each deuided with a Lilly
make them good with kind supposes
though the present be but silly

For though louelier sweetes be dwelling
in thy face so farr excelling
as twas made to make earth sweet with
yet are theise the lik'st in smelling
to thyselfe that I could meete with

Com and thou shalt tast of twenty
sortᶜ of fruit that heere in plenty
ly t'invite thee, blew dew berries
feapes [grapes?] and Damsins to content thee
Strawberries greene figgs and Cherries

With the rest this maund Ile gi' thee
caru'd and gilt to carry wi' thee
and this cupp of Box to drink on
take them in good part I preethee
though to[o] meane for thee to think on

Semple in my tongue and graces
Ill my sute yet time and place is
fitt to show thee (with small prooving)
that I am true, and that thy face is
not more faire than I am lov'ing

Aske theise Hills and Mountaines towring
Aske theise vailes and Meddowes flowreing
all will tell thee what my smart is
yf thou canst not in my showreing
eyes and sighs read whose my Hart is

The howling windes languish to se[e] me
and make each leafe murmour wi' me
Ecco plaines hir and nere sleepeth
and to view the sorrows I' me
the Night lowers and the morne weepeth

Seest thou this and canst deny me
the poore kind[n]ess to com ny me
shall wind ecco Night and morrow
heare and pitty and thou fly me
and haue no sence of my sorrow?

Ah, twill be to thee no glory
to be nam'd in my Deaths story
when thou seest it thou wilt rend it
and I know thou wilt be sorry
when twill be to[o] late to mend it.

Bod.Lib.MS.Mus.b.1,ff.88ᵛ,89.

317

Staye, staye AEneas, for thyne Owne sake staye

Staye, staye AEneas, for thyne Owne sake staye,
or Elce for myne a whyle yᵉ time delaye?
Trust not yᵉ mercye of the Raginge Seas,
and let me by degrees my greife Appease.
th'unconstant sea, and winde doe both conspire,
to giue yee what thou wantst, me my desire,
let their more Potent voice then myne thee Move,
my fault no Other is then that I loue.

"Dido to Eneas".
B.M.Loan MS. 35,f.58.

Still Amathea thou art fayre

Still Amathea thou art fayre,
    althoughe to Me
thy favors sounded but of Ayre
    sweet since from thee?
streames yt Advance from pleasinges springes,
although vnpleasant pleasure bringes.

'Twas not that looke, nor yet that dart
    from those bright Eyes
wch did Enthrall my willinge hart
    (vnhappy spies)
though not retornd and Equall boone
can ravish beautye from its Throne.

yet poore Licoris pynde for Greife
    but could not gaine
from such a Treasure a releife
    but Endles paine,
Like fond Narcissus doe I pyne
in striuinge to re-gaine what's Myne!

still thou art faire, & still as bright
    as Smyleinge Maye,
that Ads vnto our pleasinge light
    a fragrant daye.
'twas want of worth yt me deni'de
th'injoyinge of soe sweet a Bryde.

yet be not Coye, but vse yor Tyme
    roses will fade
not taken in their wonted pryme
    & in the shade
Th'enamelde Tulip wch before
Enricht each pleasant Eye prooues poore.

B.M.Loan MS.35,f.119v.

Such Lovers as shall havnt this Grove

Such Lovers as shall havnt this Grove,
to solace their delighte in Love,
and chavnce to see
this Pyramy,
an awfull reverence
be diffus'd through each sence
heere charm'd, doth lye
a Hart, by Loves nicromancy
ordain'd to show,
what fond lovers wish to know,
when Sleepe ye Harbindger of rest
is of thy Mrs eyes possest,
and thou desire
stird by Loves fire
to be sure whither she
in hir flame equall thee,
from forth ye vrne
where my tormented ashes burne
take thou a part
gently strew them on hir Heart,
which if hir colder flames susteyne
be thou assur'd she shares no paine
in thy torterings
or thy sufferings
for a fire pure as that
ought to incinerate
every member & turne each limbe
into a Cinder,
were she
to thee
Kind as mine
was crvell to me.

Bod.Lib.MS.Mus.b.1,ff.108ᵛ,109.

Sullen carre why dost thou keepe

Sullen carre why dost thou keepe
such a wa[t]ch upon hise eyes;
chasinge from them goulden sleepe,
y^t would ease his facuelties;
uanish hence as from ye light
flies ye dull abortiue night

he to whom ye surlye warre
was as natiue as his rest
by his troubled fansies far
now lies uanquish't and opres'd
gentle sleepe tis thou ma[y]st finde
a medsin for his torturd minde

Drexel MS.4041,f.10.

Sweet death com vissit my sicke hart

Sweet death com vissit my sicke hart
that loue hath soe Tormented,
prepare some phisick, show thy Art,
to cure my woes presented.
Though louers liue in highe Content,
& taste of Joye and pleasure,
I sadly sighe Out my lament,
bewayling my hard measure
now since I must yeild vp a life,
soe much (deer sweet) Ile borrow,
A graue an Epitaphe, & sighe
of you yt causd my sorrow;
soe shall my soule flye to her rest,
& liue wth Angels Euer blest.

Sweet, doe not frowne on me though I must goe

Sweet, doe not frowne on me though I must goe,
'twill rayse A storme at sea if thou doe soe,
but wth a Louely smyle be pleasd to cleere,
the weather I must haue both heer & there
what Euer wynde shall blow me from thee all in vaine,
if thou bee'st kinde my sighes shall blow me backe againe.

B.M.Loan MS.35,f.20.

Sweet I Am not Come too soone

Sweet I Am not Come too soone,
none Espyes vs but the Moone,
she her selfe hath borrow'd lyght,
to Atend On thee to Nyght;
And hath vow'de that none shall see,
what wee want but Only wee,

heer securely doe we lye
frèe from each Obseruinge Eye
blessed be that louely Godess,
wch vnites our louinge bodys
wher we kiss & none can see
what we Act but Only wee.

Joue I Enuye not thy state
though thou rule by tryple fate
I am Sealed in A Throne
worthe Ten heauens Joynd in One
where I loue & none can see
what we Act but Only wee.

Let my bosome then Conseale
that wch tongue cañot reveale
if a Joye more then devine
can be felt tis only myne
whylst I toye & none can see
what we Act but only wee.

B.M.Loan MS.35,f.18^v.

Sweet lady & sole mistres of my loue

Sweet lady & sole mistres of my loue,
Adornd wth all Rare graces from aboue,
tell me you loiall Servant wherfore you,
to whose perfections greatest prayse is due
doe vse to him yts yors to change yor fashion,
somtimes from louinge kindnes into passion.

is it to trye how firme my loue was fix't
my hopes with feares must thus be intermix't
Or is't to shew how yor sweet smile or frowne
Can raise a louer vp or cast him downe,
what e're it be, that makes you sometimes strange
There's nought can make my loue decrease or change.

Sweet wātton wagg whose chaire of state

Sweet wātton wagg whose chaire of state
is mounted in my mistries eyes
ffrom whence thow shotte an arrow late
in brest of her dred diety :
oh pitty me oh pitty me.

Sweetest Cloris lend a kisse

Sweetest Cloris lend a kisse
the more you spare the lesse you misse
were it two, were it three were it ten
they may be ouer done agen
And when breathlesse you Can noe More
you May be sure of all my store

learne betimes liuing loues Misterie
weel finde out still varietye
tis Ignorance that makes you Coy
to fly from what you'd faine injoy
Tis Louers food, tis bewtyes Charme
seales up our loue and keepes it warme

Consider too that youth might wast
Hast Cloris and redeeme whats past
Loose noe tyme, in your prime for when you'r old
Men Neglect and loue grows Cold
Best Apetites are soonest starud
and such is myne if not preserud.

Kisse, tis bewtyes food affections Charme
Seales up our Loue and keeps it warme.

B.M.Add.MS.31432,front fly leaf.

Tarry sweete love

Tarry sweete love
harke how the winds doe murmure at yor fflyghte
See how the trees in order growe
the coole earth shadoinge belowe
see the wanton streames how they playe by the banke side.
Then Stay
in hope my lighte
my Joye my life my soule heere may you safe aBide.

Ch.Ch.439,f.2.

Taught from yᵒʳ Artfull straines my faire

Taught from yor Artfull straines my faire,
I Euer since haue liu'de by Ayre;
whose sounds doe make me wish I were
either all voice or elce all Eare.

if soules (as some saye) Musique be
I'ue learnt from you ther's one in me,
from you whose Accents make vs know
that sweeter sphaeres moue heer below.

from you whose limbes are soe well mett
that we may sweare yor body's sett,
whose parts are wth such graces Crownd
that tis but Musique wthout sound.

I had in part, this loue before
but you awakde, & made it more,
as when a gentle Euninge showre
cals foorth, & Ads, scent to ye flowre.

Hencfoorth Ile thinke my breath is due
noe more to Nature but to you!
singe I to pleasure then or fame
Ile know noe Anthemne but yor Name.

this shall Joye life, this sweeten death
you that haue taught, may clayme my breath.

B.M.Loan MS.35,f.120.

Teares doe not spare

Teares doe not spare
mine eyes, they doe no more
then serve my Harts affliction to deplore

Sighes doe not spare
my Hart yts growne to be,
stranger to all things but Callamitie,

Groanes Doe not spare
my Brest and tongue yt fare
better with yu, then Mirth acquainted are,

Teares sighe and groanes,
let me not frendlesse dye,
for none but yrs is frendly company.

Tell hir he yᵗ sent hir this

Tell hir he yᵗ sent hir this,
nor lustfull nor Love f[r]antique is,
but in true Judgement did celect,
hir vnto whom all ow respect,
yf she obiect thou wantest Art,
say tis the language of his hart
that knew 'twas easier to discry,
twixt truth of Love and Poetry,
This this with sighes expresse, and then
sweare that his thoughte outspeake his Pen.

Tell me no more of Giues of Brasse

Tell me no more of Giues of Brasse
thy Bolts are libertye
nor art thou bound fond slaue soe fast
but gold may ransome thee
Yet wert thou helpless still thy minde
Can in no prison be Confin'd

See'st thou vaine foole this Single hayre
More fine then Sunbeames farr ;
It was a glorious ray that Crown'd
Once my propitious Starre.
'Twas her delight, but now my paine
And tyes me faster then thy Chaine.

Tis true my liueinge Scelleton
May freely walke the round
But yet the Soule that makes ye man
Is to one Center bound.
Soe Sunbeames through the ayre doe glide
Yet with the Suñ they still abide.

Hopeless I lye nor can I finde
a price that may redeeme my minde
Lass? Can he hope for libertye
whose Gaoler must his ransome be
Thou hat'st thy prison. I mine loue
for freedome would my bondage proue.

Had vulcan sett soe rich a Ginne
Soll had bin proud t'haue bin Kept in.

B.M.Add.MS.29396,ff.33ᵛ-5.

Tell me noe more tis loue

Tell me noe more tis loue,
    yor passions moue
in a fantasticke sphaere,
    and only there
thus you confine
    what is devine
when loue hath powre & can dispence
sufficient to the soule & sence.

'Tis loue the Sence informes
    & cold blood warmes
nor giues ye soule A Throne
    to rule Alone
but bids them bend
    both to one End ;
And then tis loue, when thus designd
they make an Other of their kinde.

B.M.Loan MS.35,f.62ᵛ.

Tell mee shepherd dost y^u love?

Nymph   : Tell mee shepherd dost y^u love?

Shepherd : Tell mee Nimph why would'st y^u know:

Nymph   : Thy wandringe flock y^t w^thout guide doth Rove,
                 thy Blubbred Eyes y^t still wth teares o're flow,
                 makes mee to aske. S : I doe.

Nymph   : deere shepherd tell mee whoe

Shepherd : I love a Nymph from whose faire Eyes
                 Phoebus doth his brightnes borrow,
                 where love did first my hart surprize,
                 wch since hath caus'd my sorrow.

Nymph   : Love sitts inthron'd w^thin ye Circle of bright Eyes,
                 but say (good shepherd) doe her Vertues beauties
                      Equallize.

Shepherd : As shee in beauty doth all else Excell,
                 So are her Vertues w^thout all Paralell.

Nymph   : Doth shee disdayne y^ee, *S* ; No, *N* : Why greiu'st
                 thou then.

Shepherd : Because her love is onely worthy of the Gods, not Men.

N & S   : Loves cheifest ioye is but a pleasinge Anguish,
                 Who liues in love doth dyeing liue, & living languish.

B.M.Add.MS.11608,ff.18^v,19^v.

That flame is borne of Earthly fire

That flame is borne of Earthly fire
that soone enjoies and soone expires
his loue wth wings ill featherd flyes,
yt Cañot reach beyond his Eyes.

Though Alps and Ocons bould devide
the shepeard from his sweetharts side
Loue has a trick, a pritty Art
to Cary loue from hart to hart

Wher hope doth fan the Idle fyer
tis Easy to Maintayne desire
but thats the loue yt nobly dare
Continew Constant in dispaire.

B.M.Add.MS.31432, f.36.

The Catts as other creatures doe

The Catts as other creatures doe
use oft to swagger when they woe
and in the darke and coldest night
yes Jefry lions use to fight
then they cry mew and so they fearce
on both sides Joyne
and cry who teares thy coate and mine
thou & I thus they cry mew :
still they cry mew.

But o the crewelst battel far
was fought last night att temple barr
whereon the tiles oth houses ther
Sir boare Catt bold was heard to sweare

The slaue yt coms to my pus shall dye
to whome sir sharp nayle giues ye lye
and with clawes fiue set on his face
in bloody Charecters disgrace
Then they cry mew for which affront
they both sides iones
and cry who teares thy coate & mine
thou and I thus they cry mew :
still they cry mew.

And whilst these two dispute the cause
pus being much affrighted mews
and Cals for helpe to part the fray
whose voyce the nebouring catts obey

And thicke and threefold in a trice
they theither came & left the mice
to sporte and play for all pretend
there pusses honour theile defend.

336

for nine liued Catt that neuer knew
what pale feare ment his weapons drew
which when sir Catt A mountaine saw
he one his visage layde his pawe
and those two likewise fearcely Joynd
and cry who teares thy coate & mine
thou & I thus they cry mew :
still they cry mew.

The higeous noyse & blowes increace
and whilst most fought some would keepe peace
but they no Constable regard
kings Cruce nor Justice is not heard
for they cry mew ; still they cry mew.
The Catts that are of the⌢ins of court
they thought att first itt had bin sport
and so the hungry blades came there
in hopes they might haue gott good Cheare

But when sir kill Catt spies them out
he secretly informd the Rout
that they came out to draw an action
to uex them with the lawes distraction
to hinder this there falce designe
letts cry who teares thy coate & mine
thou & I thus they cry   Mew.

Drexel MS.4041,ff.115ᵛ-116ᵛ.

The drowzy Night hir wings has spred

1.   The drowzy Night hir wings has spred
    like sable curtaines 'bout each Head,
    & woes yᵉ weary Limbs to Bedd,

2.   The Sun with toyle and Heat opprest,
    is long since sunke vnto hir rest,
    and cooles his flames on Thetis breast.
    And now pale Cynthia rides yᵉ round
    wᵗʰ Dyadems of silver crown'd
    to awe yᵉ spirrits vndergrovnd

1&2 May hir dread scepter from yoᵘ keepe
    all horrid objects yᵗ wovld creepe,
    amongst yᵉ quiets of yʳ sleepe
    And she hir pretty Fayries bring
    to charme yᵘ faster while they Sing
    and in yʳ fancy daunce their Ring

1.   Thus may yoᵘ revell out the Night
    till Titan reasume his right
    and play about yoᵘ wᵗʰ new light.

1&2 While Little Robin Dead Mens freind,
    who sadly did yʳ Corpse attend
    and thought yoʳ sleepe had bine yoʳ end,
    Seeing Morphevs gin to slack his chaine,
    shall rowze yᵘ wᵗʰ a cheerfull straine
    ore joy'd to find yoᵘ live againe.

Bod.Lib.MS.Mus.b.1,ff.161v,162,162v.

The first concoction perfited

The first concoction perfited
when wanton fumes were made
the fancyes theame
my Mists came vnto my Bed
transhap't into a Dreame,

Shee stood as naked and as white as Snow,
not Jove more Beavty covld bestowe
on the faire Swan's beloved skin
Nor Venus could more softnes showe
Shovld she put on hir Clovd ag'in.

The God of loue my shepperd is

The God of loue my shepperd is,
& he y^t doth me feed,
whylst he is Myne And I am his,
what can I want or Need;
he leades me to ye tender grass,
wher I both feed & rest,
then to ye streames that gently pass,
in both I haue ye best.

Or if I stray, he doth Convert
and bringe my Mynde in frame
And All this not for My desert
but for his Holye Name:
yea, in deathles shadie black Abode
well may I walk, not feare
for thou Art wth me, And thy rod
to guide, thy staffe to beare.

Nay thou doost make me sitt & dyne
Eu'n in Myne Enimies sight
my Head wth Oyle, my Cup wth wyne
Ruñs Ouer daye and night;
Surely thy sweet & wondrous Loue
shall Measure all my daies
And as it Never shall remove
soe Neither shall my praise.

B.M.Loan MS.35,f.77.

340

The hower is come in wch I must resigne

Man   : The hower is come in wch I must resigne
            to Dust what tyme and willing nature made
            so long my sovles flesh shade,
            Man is a poore and vndone thing,
            when his Imortall part is taking wing.
            But whether wilt thou fly my Sperrit

Divell : Without a Merrit

Man   : What voice is yt a suddain feare
            doth wound my trembling Eare,

Divell : Know thy accuser foole tis I,

Man   : what killing Horror doth invade my Eye,
            Mercy oh Mercy.

Divell : Tis to[o] late
            ye Judge is sate,
            nor canst thou fly

Man   : Oh let me hide
            me in his Crimson side
            yt died
            for Man *Divell* : There is no roome
            yt wound was never made to be thy Tombe,

Man   : Is there no Balme *Divell* : No Balme for thee,

Man   : Although it be
            to ye proportion of a teare,
            Let but that drope appeare,
            One little drope would purge my Sinn,
            And turne my Sperritt to a Seraphin,

Divell : Heaven is no Arke nothing can there
            defil'd appeare,

Man   : But tis ye Chamber of ye Bride,
            are Pleasures there denied

Divell : To them yt wast theire tyme and light,
            Therfore make hast and come away tis Night,

Angell : Looke vp sad soale with Milky wing
a Dove doth bring
An Olive branch as to y^t Boate
when ye Old world did floate
wth all theire Magazine to shew
y^t now ye angry tide of Heaven is low

Man : What doe I see streame throug[h] ye Aire,

Divell : Thy own dispaire
Do not expect when it is Darke,
to save thy Sea torne Barke.

Angell : Fly hence black fiend and let it Swim
thou flingst false Clouds betwixt my Beames and him
Arise and see ye blood-staind Crosse

Divell : Foole tis thy losse

Angell : There naile thy selfe be Crucified
with ye sweet Lamb y^t dyed,
He y^t was Preist and sacrifize,
Shall sna[t]ch thy panting Soale to Paradice,

Man : Shoot vp my faith, *Angell* : Thy signe display

Divell : Throw it away

Man : Arme me O Jesu in this warr,
where wound℮ ye Trivmph are

Divell : I find my malice strucken lame,
And Hell doth tremble at that glorivs name

Angell&
Man : Looke how ye Serpent on his Belly creepes
to hide him in Eternall deepes
while we Bath in full streames of Blisse
beyond what flowed in Paradice,
yet theise are Rillets to those Seas above,
wch drowne blest sowles in Everlasting love.

Bod.Lib.MS.Mus.b.1,ff.153ᵛ-156ᵛ.

The mary gould of golden hew

The mary gould of golden hew
obesiance owes vnto the Sunn
she spreads abroad her leaves to vew
when phebus ginns his course to Runn
and for that honour shee doth shewe
shee hath rewarde allwaies to growe

But when the sunne hath Runn her race :
and all at rest that earst had paine :
she close her leaves and hides her face :
till phebus light appeares againe :
then as her wonte with gladsome cheere
vnto the Sunne shee doth appeere.

My mary goulde soe favours me :
my presence onelie doth her glad :
When I am gonn right well I See :
in chamber close shee sitts as Sad :
As did for wante of her delight :
Penelope that wofull wighte :

Then for rewarde till life shall ende :
my pen and tongue shall shewe her praise :
My hand her honour shall defende :
my hart shall love her all my daies :
this guifte I geue her as vnknowne :
I will be hers and not my owne :

Ch.Ch.MS.439,ff.9ᵛ,10.

The patterne often drawne in minde

The patterne often drawne in minde
appeares in flesh & fills mine eye
If any Scratch therin I finde,
'tis but a MarKe to owne it by
More wealth or beautye losse would bee,
& maKe my Choice too good for mee,
        who must loue thee.

Now Since an Obiect I haue gain'd
Wheron to sett & fix my heart
My wandringe thoughts are all restrain'd
I feele no RacK of doubtfull Smart
I would not for a Kingdome be
Redeem'd from this Captiuitye
        Of loueing thee

What forme So e're I now looKe on,
fatt, Leane, Tall, Short, Young, neuer Old
The gentle fayre, the witty browne
The CrooKed streightned with her gold
All One or Pictures seeme to mee
Because I haue noe eyes to see
        More Loues then thee.

The Glasse one shaddow doth Containe
The wax one Print, my hart one Loue;
A flaminge fire, to fire againe
Or light the day-light who will proue?
Through burninge beauties I goe free
No Amorous flame can seaze on mee
        Inflam'd by thee.

Loue mee by leasure as you may,
Tis great Content that I loue you
Glutt not my soule with quick repay
Vnlesse to ease yr doubtinges too.
With single Loue Ile feed my breast
That so on double it may feast
            When yo loue mee
                        mee best.

B.M.Add.MS.29396,ff.28ᵛ,29.

The sad Nymph, Gaho, followed to the shadie woods

The sad Nymph, Gaho, [Echo?] followed to the shadie woods,
belou'de Narcissus but belou'de of her in vayne,
And in a vale bedecte with sundrie flowry buds,
shee heares him at a fountaine side him selfe to playne :
    hee sight and soe did shee,
    and whiles hee cries
        Ay mee :
  the trembling Ecchoe cries againe.

You cristall streames quoth hee that in your glassie face,
Present a forme soe rich, soe pure, soe past compare,
Why hath the vper streames the lower thus in chase ?
Are they phaps caught allso with my bewties steare ? :
    ffly not so fast away,
    Narcissus cryes ô stay :
        ô stay.
  Poore Ecchoe cryes but in despaire.

Twas not for nought yt Nymphe stood silent in a gaze,
As if the Sonne had shot his beames from out his eyes,
The substance sure must make the louer in a maze
When now such force, such flames, such fier in th'image lyes :
    Ø giue, cryes Narcissus,
    To coole the heate one kisse :
        one kisse,
  Shrill Ecchoe from the woods replyes.

Hee kiss'de but more did burne, yet for to quench the flame,
Hee kisde againe, againe the kisse enflamde his blood,
Till all on fier, hee needes must then imbrace the same,
And springs with open armes into the fatall flood
    But ôh I dye, hee cryes,
    Alas I dye : hee dyes,
       hee dyes,
  And leaues poore Ecchoe in the wood.

Drexel MS.4175,XXII.

The simple Bee yt do's no harme

The simple Bee yt do's no harme
may make me arme
my selfe from yt vnmanly Ill,
a sloathfull will,
and learne from Natures husbandman
(in this lifes span)
the ever busy-thriveing Ant,
how to shun want;
for by their labour I perceiue
they not bereave
theire pretious selves with tyme ill spent,
yt they repent;
I yt am made of Creatures best,
thinke on it least,
for where shall any find a freind
to last to th'end.
This though I knowe and Inly sorrow,
doe worse tomorrow.
To greeve, and yet doe Ill, wee se[e] is ever then
like one yt Climbs ye highest tree to fall agen.

The Turtle is a simple byrde

The Turtle is a simple byrde,
but syllier Farr are they
whoe pyne not Only for a death,
but for what straies awaye
giue me the Independent Soule,
whose self is its cheife Joye,
freely Entertaines & freely leaues
defy'inge the blinde boye
such phebes Jolly Freedome is
as blythe at a depart
as when shee meets whom best shee likes
none comes too neere her hart
let them be gone ye loss is theirs,
is all shee sayes & all shee Cares.

B.M.Loan MS.35,ff.169ᵛ,170.

The wound Love gave me th'other day

The wound Love gave me th'other day
my Soule with anguish doth so fill
I Knowe not in what place to stay,
Death were a Kindnesse would it Kill,

so foule a shott was never made
at any tender Heart before,
but if this be thy bloudy trade,
thy Temples I'le adore no more,

thy ould acquaintance sure is Ceast,
with Heartę that gentlenes doe Know,
and dwells in som cold Scythian brest
yᵗ could deserve so bovld a blowe,

no Cupid there's no Noble Heart,
but does it selfe to Love incline,
nor need'st thou home to draw thy Dart,
to punnish those whose sovles are thine,

A slight scra[t]ch from thy Mothers hand
will make them bleede and swoune away,
when vnder heartę yᵗ force wᵗʰstand
and will not all thy power obey.

Bod.Lib.MS.Mus.b.1,ff.174ᵛ,175,175ᵛ.

There is a thing y^t much is us'd

There is a thing y^t much is us'd
tis called Love by men abus'd
They write they sigh & sweare they Dye
w^n all is done they know they Lye
But let y^m sweare by faith & Troth
Ile sweare they can not for an Oath.

They first must have a M^{rs} faire
And y^n a favour for to weare
And then they goe to flattreys school
And call her wise they know's a foole :
But let y^m sweare by faith & Troth
Ile sweare they can not for an Oath

There is a practise in this Age
They lay theire creditts unto gage
By will by vowes by neat Attire
To conquer y^t they most desire :
But let y^m sweare by faith & Troth
Ile sweare they can not for an Oath.

Since yn y^t all theire thoughts are vaine
Since fancy rules theire hearts by fitts
Since they are fond & falce by kind
Since to delude they worke by fitts
Since they are carlesse of their Troth
Never to love Ile take an Oath.

There was a froge swum In the lake

There was a froge swum In the lake
the crab came crawlinge by
wilte thow coth the froge be my mate
coth the crab noe noe not I
my skin is sooth [smooth] & dapled fine
I can leape farre & nye
thy shell is hard soe is not mine
coth the crab noe noe not I

Tell me then spake the crab therefore
or els I thee defye
give me thy claw I aske noe more
coth the froge & that will I
the crab bitt of the frogs fore feete
the froge then he muste dye
to wooe a crab it is not meete
If any doe it is not I.

Ch.Ch.MS.439,ff.6ᵛ,7.

These hands shall beate vpon my pensiue brest

These hands shall beate vpon my pensiue brest
And sad to death, for sorrow rent my hayre
my voyce to call on thee shall neur rest
Thy grace I seeke, thy Judgment I do feare
vpon ye ground all groueling on my face
Lord I beseech thy fauour & thy grace

Thy mercy greatr is then any sinne
thy greatnes none could eur cōprhend,
wherefore good lord let me thy mercy winne
whose glorious name no tyme can eur ende
Then shall I sing with thyne elect in heauen
Thy prayse & powr world wthout ende Amen.

Tenbury Wells MS.1019, fly leaf.

This day our Sauior Christ was born

This day our Sauior Christ was born;
att bethlem in a Com̃on Inn;
on Caluary was his body torn
to paij ye payn ye ransom, of our Sinn:
Nay from ye manger to the Cross
he mad his Lif a mystick story
& of his blod hee thought no loss
to bring his enemies to glory;
his Lif hath buried all our Sinns,
his death our endles Glorie winnes,
Then Let vs Caroll to his prays
the Choisest of our holy Layes
& thus Inflamd with melting fiere;
ye Saints will Chant it, in our quire.

Tenbury Wells MS.1018, f.9ᵛ.

this merry pleasant springe

this merry pleasant springe
harke how the sweete birde singes
& carall in the tops & one the bryer
Jug Jug Jug the Nightingall deliuers
yt it it it the sparowes sings his hott desire
the Robin he recordes the larke quiuers
sweet as sweete as ever
from straines soe sweet birds deprive vs never.

Those Heau'nly Rayes of thyne

Those Heau'nly Rayes of thyne
wch in thy face doe shyne,
are to Enforme, & let vs see,
what rare perfection is in thee;
    none will or maye,
    not thinke I say,
this of thee to increase thy fame,
since thou Art best knowne by thy name.

The Fayrest will not deeme
themselues faire nor Esteeme
theyr beauties wch they will not Owne
wth out some likenes to thyne Owne
    nor yet wth all
    will the best call
their vertues soe, except they see
thy vertues their paterne to be.

When all is saide & done
thy Lustre like the sun
All beauties doth Excell as farr
As the Suñ A plañet or starr;
    And this alwaies
    shall be thy praise
thou all Excellest, and that none
like thy selfe is but thou aLone.

B.M.Loan MS.35,f.172 "On the Lady AñePercy".

Those Louers only Hapye are

Those Louers only Hapye are
that still dispaire
the Restlesse soules that hope and Feare,
in Tempests liue each smyle or frowne,
like Surges Tosse them vpp and downe,
and if they Ere
attain the Port, they shipwrack ther,
and sink their loue though they Escape,
For bewtye shape,
and all those sweets wch they before,
did with soe much delight adore
if Tasted they esteeme noe More,
and Once enjoyed
they ar noe sooner pleasd then Cloyd,
But he that dares his hart preffer
to worship her
whose Eyes deuine fyre doth not burne
but all Loue into Wonder turne,
Blest in his Objects Glories are,
and ther dispaire
secures that blisse from all Impaire.

B.M.Add.MS.31432,ff.46ᵛ :47.

Thou art heau'n Olimpia

Thou art heau'n Olimpia,
Ossa on Pelion
wee Riuall Giants laye,
in vaine to Scale thy Throne.
Encelladus wth Thunder struck,
Buried in Ashes lyes,
vnder a Flameinge Rock
the Trophy of thyne Eyes.

Thou by yᵉ pleasant springe shalt lye

Thou by yᵉ pleasant springe shalt lye,
list'ning to birds sweet mellodye,
whyle Satyres, & vpstartinge fawnes
doe sport it on yᵉ fragrant lawnes.
Graunt ledia but to be my loue,
weele tyre delight, all pleasures proue.

yᵉ Goddes of yᵉ groue for thee
shall Charme delight on Eurye tree
and beautious Flora shall Combine
garlands about thy head to twyne
the first fruits shalbe due to thee
in token of thy deitye.

Then at the foot of Some greene Hill
wee'le lye & heer sweet phillomell
mourne for her loue, whylst watry bubles
prompt vs to rest sweet balme for troubles
and Turtle doues lull vs asleepe
whose sad sweet notes makes joye to weepe.

B.M.Loan MS.35,f.10.

Thov dreges of Lethey ô thov dull

Thov dreges of Lethey ô thov dull :
vnhospitable Jvice of hvll :
not to bee drank but in the divels skull.

depriued of those sollid Joyes :
yᵗ sack creates Avthor of noyes :
Among ye roraioing pungqves and dam mee boyes :

one thy accovnt the watch dos sleepe
when they ovr nightly peace shovld keepe :
Then Roagves and cvtpvrse in at windows creepe.

The ivgg broke pate doth owe to thee
His bloodie lyne and pedigree
now mvrdvr and anon the gallow tree

A poette once did lick thy ivyce
but ô how his bemoned mvse
did myre in nonsence and base state abvse

A sovldoer one yᵗ would haue pickt
strife with ye divel thy dvll broth lickt
that night this renownd tvrdivant was kickt.

Tother night twas ye mealeman will
did lapp soe largly of thy swill
next morne hee lett a fart blew downe his mill

That lover was in pretty case
that trymde thee with a ginger race
and after belcht thee in his mistres face

more of thy virtves I could tell
bvt to think of thee is halfe hell
heere take thy cvrse by candle book & bell.

360

may bardes whoe drinke thee write a small
vnsvbstanct Lyne pedanticall
vnsinnved senselese enigmaticall

faultlesse and gavlles bee't thy curse
nvmberles emptie ragged wors
then the poor poets dowblett belly purs

May hee that breves thee weare a noase
reader then the lordmaieres Cloathes
the sattin cherrie or the vellvit roas

May hee that drawes thee lickewyse ware
a carbungkell from eare to eare
that thatch and linnon may stand off and feere

May som owld hagg witch gitt astrid
thy bvng as if shee meant to ride
and bvng to bvng ovtlantt thy yesttie tide

May others bee bvt sick as I
that sooke thee next then downe and dye
Poor alle a fvnarall tray for wasp and fly

Drexel MS.4041,ff.67ᵛ,68.

Thou that spendst thy time to knowe

Thou that spendst thy time to knowe
whether shee can love or noe
y^t canst love hir cruelty
better then hir liberty,
Come come away
I can noe longer stay,
By those powers I invoke thee,
wch to love did first provoke thee,
by those charming eyes of hers
by the severall formes and stirrs
wch hir scornes wrought in thy Heart
By all the follyes all hir Art,
by the pretty braided twist,
and the Bracelet on thy wrist
By that small enameld Ring,
and y^t wch holds it safe ye string,
by ye gentle Networke purse
wch if lost must be thy curse,
By the Riban in thy locke,
and all Cupids pedling stocke,
I charge thee to appeare,
an See Doctor I am heere.

though cupit be a god

though cupit be a god
alas hese but a boy
and Venus who he mother calles
we all knowe for A toy

Theres no such thing as loue
that dares now to appeare :
grate marce himselfe hath gin it ouer
and is turnd Cauilier

What wonder is it then
if ladies here belowe
are left alone to make their mone
and sing hinoninoe

Se how they ride and run
to lay hold on A man
sum pul sum Crie som sware thele dye
yet not A thing will stande

Wel in A rag they sware
they all will roundheads bee
for then the Cauiliers Agin
will at them furiously.

Drexel MS.4041,f.38.

Though my Bodye be restraind

Though my Bodye be restraind
from thy presence, yet my mynde,
wth Fetters can be chaynd,
but a passage it will find
to thy Bosome, where ye bliss,
of my Soule enclosed is.

what are these disasters then
liue I bound or liue I free
cares like shaddowes vanish when
I doe feed my thoughts on thee!
On thy will my life depends
that my joye or Sorrow Ends!

Then devinest beautyes wonder
let our soules Embrace each Other
though or bodys liue asunder
and let noe Affliction smoother
that sweet flame whose sacred fyre
Cupids swoons shall not Expire.

B.M.Loan MS.35,f.83ᵛ.

Though yᵒ determine not to Loue

Though yo determine not to Loue
Yet ciuill you might bee,
yʳ scuruye slightinges onely moue,
an equall scorne in mee
who sue not on yᵉ Beggers score,
to take an answer at the dore.

You thinke, vnlesse yo first ore'come
My passion wᵗʰ your pride
It will in time grow troublesome
And hardly bee deny'd :
Haue patience ! I'le secure yʳ feare
'Tis not soe greiuous to forbeare.

Or else by seeminge strangely Nice
you may pretend to make
your Chapman sett the higher price,
faith then you much mistake.
for such as meane to sell their ware
Though they aske high, had need speak fayre.

I take it, 'twill not bee your turne
to conquer by disdaine
And to Massacre wᵗʰ a scorne ;
More wisely then refraine ;
Least Hee, to whom it is adrest
proue vnconcern'd, & spoile yᵉ Jest.

B.M.Add.MS.29396,ff.62ᵛ,63.

Though you on seas in stormes haue bin

Though you on seas in stormes haue bin,
And seene their foame when Billowes meet,
And though you haue both felt & seene,
ye silke-wormes graue, or wyndinge sheet ;
though you haue suckt in Indian wynde,
that hath kist ten Thousand leaues of Cynom trees,
their Gums, their Rynde, all wch of sweetnes it bereaues,
yet you will saye, theres nought can be
whyte, softe or sweet that is not she.

B.M.Loan MS.35,f.23ᵛ.

Thus dark sett of my light, wch like a Ray

Thus dark sett of[f] my light, wch like a Ray,
shot through black Clovds strikes from ye Midnight day
when ye rough windes conspire and waues engage
I stand a Rock vnmooved to all theire Rage,
So Palmes deprest, advance theire enuy'd height,
and vertue gathers by his Curb and weight
Vanity, Grace, Glory three Crownes held forth,
truth taught mee a distinction of their worth,
The first was gay, but heauy to be worne,
The second sharp, but light, a Crowne of thorne,
The third a blessed and Eternall one
wth beames of Beatifique vision,
The trifle of this world becoms ye ground
of my contempt nor can ye second wound,
with all hir speares my patient Hand, by grace
of my Redeemer whose first wreath it was,
In Heaven my soule beheld ye last, and I,
enioy, what hope lookt for, Eternity.

Bod.Lib.MS.Mus.b.1,ff.157,157ᵛ,158.

Thus sang Orpheus to his strings

Thus sang Orpheus to his strings
wn he was almost slaine
while ye winds soft murmurings
Eccho'd all his woes againe
Euridice Euridice he cry'd
Ah deare Euridice & so he dy'de
Euridice, Ah deare Euridice
ye Ecchoing winde reply'd

His head in ye water fell,
And wth soft voice seemd to sing
Death could not his musick quell.
Ev'ry wave strook Ev'ry string
Euridice Euridice it cry'd
Ah deare Euridice & so it dyed
Euridice ah! deare Euridice
The sounding bank reply'd.

'tis but a frowne, I prithee let me dye

'tis but a frowne, I prithee let me dye,
One Bended brow, Concludes my Tragidye.
for all my loue, I begg but this of thee ;
thou wilt not be, too longe in killinge me
for since you loue not, what avayles yor smyle ;
you Onlye warme a ball of Snow ye whyle ;
wch whylst it gathers comfort from yr Eyes,
wth that same Comfort, Melts awaye, & dyes.
thus in the End, yor frownes, & smyles are One,
& differ but in execution.

B.M.Loan MS.35,f.48ᵛ.

Tis Christmas now, 'tis Christmas now

Tis Christmas now, 'tis Christmas now
when Cato's selfe would laugh
& smoothinge foorth his wrinckled brow
giue libertye to Quafe
to daunce, to singe, to sport & playe
for Eurye Howre's a Hollidaye.

As for the Twelfe dayes let y^{em} pass
in myrth & Jollitye
ye tyme doth call each lad & lass
y^t will be blyth & merry
to daunce, to singe, to sport & playe
for Eurye Howre's a Hollidaye.

And as for venus let her be
part of our recreation
A wench or soe in Jollitye
was never yet damnation
then daunce & singe & sport & playe
for Eurye Howre's a Hollidaye.

And from ye kiseinge of ye suñ
wth settinge cast of cares
tis tyme Enough when Twelfe is done
to thinke of our Affaires
Then daunce & singe & sport & playe
for Eurye Howre's a Hollidaye.

B.M.Loan MS.35,f.31.

Tis noe shame to yeild

Tis noe shame to yeild
to beauty that still wiñes the feild
the god of warr could not resist
her charge nor hercules persist
in conquest but did captiue lye
surprizd by Omphales fayer ey
the wise the valiant rich discrete
feeling her power fall prostrate at her feete

Armd in her selfe if she appeare
the sauing sheilds y e sword y e speare
are Charmd out of the victors hand
and they as liueleese statures stand
the wise the valiant rich discrete
feeling her power fall prostrate at her feete

Why then since there is no defence
against such persing victorie
should weake men striue in vaine
being borne to bee
vassals to women and y r soueranity
the wise the valiant rich discrete
feeling her power fall prostrate at her feete

Drexel MS.4041,ff.80,80 ᵛ.

Tis not Boy thy Amorous looke

1   : Tis not Boy thy Amorous looke,
      though far more Cleerer then ye brooke
      Wherin NarCissus buried was,
      Nor yet thy all aluring face
      soe takes my hart, but lyes Confynd,
      within the Circle of thy mynde,

2   : But thy two peircing beames attracts,
      More then the God of loue exacts ;

1   : Thy Grace doth Add vnto a deity

2   : Thy lookes teacheth us Peitye
      And heere devinest let me lye,
      sau'd by loue, ore slayne by your Eye

1   : Ay me, Ay me, but Can thy Vowes be as they seeme

2   : As true, as thou Out shinst loues Queene.

1&2 : Then for our Offerings let us bring,
      Chast and virginall flames and Sing.
      Thanks to the Gods yt thus hath woue
      Harts into Eyes soules into loue.

B.M.Add.MS.31432,ff.27ᵛ,28.

Tis not the world not what can please

Tis not the world not what can please,
with vaine delights (the soules disease)
I care to loose,
for if the fates first call me
to that bliss whither wee
both shall goe, I cannot chuse,
nor doe I greeve
those joyes to leave,
wch we in femalls doe conceave

I ioy'd ym never,
nor doe I feare to pass the shade
of cruell Death, for who is made,
to live heere ever.
But ô I dye before I dye,
to thinke that we
twixt whom there is such simpathy,
should parted be.

Bod.Lib.MS.Mus.b.1,ff.49ᵛ,50.

Tis not thy well-mixd Red & whyte

Tis not thy well-mixd Red & whyte,
      that can invite
into Loues bands my Free-borne soule,
could beauty' in all her charmes, surprize
my warye hart or wiñ myne eies,
      thy pow're were done
& Persian-Like I'de Court the morninge suñ.

'tis not thy vertue nor thy witt,
      that wee submit
& midst thy meaner Captiues stand :
if Nun-like thoughts frozen desires,
could nourish or had bred my fyres?
      I'de Leaue thy face,
& in myne Armes some virgin Lilly place.

Elinda yet thy soule I loue,
      but thence remoue,
they wel-becominge pryde, and then
I'me lost ; the glories ye delight,
tis that both makes & Crownes ye Fight,
      resolue, I dy
in ye persuite, but couldst thou yeild, Ide Flye.

B.M.Loan MS.35,ff.180,180ᵛ.

To Man that was i'th Eu'ninge mad

To Man that was i'th Eu'ninge mad,
starrs gaue the first delight,
Admyreinge in the gloomy shade,
those little drops of light;
Then at Aurora whose fayre hand
re-moou'd them from ye skies,
he gazinge Tow'rd the East did stand,
she Entertaind his Eyes.
but when the bright Suñ did Appeere
All these he gan dispise,
his wonder was determynd there,
and could noe higher Rise,
he neither might, nor wish'd to know,
a more Refulgent light,
for that as myne yor beautyes now,
Imployde his vtmost Syght.

To those whose bosomes harbours woes

To those whose bosomes harbours woes
soft pillowes marble seeme to be,
but flints seeme feathers vnto those
whose happy harts of cares are free
Nor silke nor songs beget sweete sleepe,
nor hearbes nor spices Can it make
nor bed of stone, or stubble keepe
the free and happy hart awake
But in close couch of mans one brest
is lodg'd his waking or his rest.

Yet let no ioyes to[o] much secure
Thy silly thoughts from prudent feare
since sleepe once past thou art not sure
To find thy pleasures where they weare
As ship is now on surges tost
That earst did sayle on quiet streame
O how much price and hope is lost
in shorter moment then a dreame
Keepe then to breake thy bodies rest
A wakefull mind in sleeping brest.

Ch.Ch.MS.Mus.87,ff.16ᵛ,17.

To whome shall I Complaine, to Men or Gods

To whome shall I Complaine, to Men or Gods,
noe both ar Joynd and still with mee at Odds,
They Make my hart the Anvill of their blow
Forming each day New and Tormenting Woes,
Breake Hart and make them Crueller then wise,
for by yir Tyranie, their Triumph dyes.

B.M.Add.M S.31432,f.22.

Transcendent Beauty though y^u art

Transcendent Beauty though y^u art
light to mine eyes life to my heart
& in whose beauty rests alone
the only true philosophers stone
for as th'Elixar can restore
Nature decay'd as was before
thy power hath wrought a stranger thing
by changing Autumne into Spring.

Treade Junos steps who list for me

Treade Junos steps who list for me,
I Joye in my virginitie
and still a mayden will remaine
attendinge on Dianas trayne

Sylvanus wood & pleasant [s]pringe
I will not leave to have a kinge
my virgins care I vowed to have
Vntoucht to bringe me to my grave.

What neede wee wedd & maye goe free
Dyana oft hathe warned me
that many Cares depende thereon
& therfore husbands will I non.

a Care the husband to Content
I am nowe free Ile not Consent
a Care lest he defraude his wife
I list not so to leade my lyfe.

B.M.Add.MS.15117, f.15ᵛ.

Troth ladye Ile not court y too't

Troth ladye Ile not court ye too't
much less pay excise for venery
& plunge my selfe in penury
   youle not supply :
when flesh and quine decrease.
purchasd loue can neuer last
loathed Tis as soone as past
   all know itt
though ye excessiue fyre remaines
with siluer bellowes asts & paines [corruption of O.E. blæst?]
   to blow itt
I would not for the world for court or woe
at once to be lauish & seruile to :

Drexel MS.4041,ff.51-52.

'Twas not his person nor his partes

'Twas not his person nor his partes,
though ne're soe fam'd that wonn mee.
Hee lou'd hee sayd, wch I beleiu'd,
and y^t fayth hath vndone mee
His vertues were alike to all
nor were they more to mee
I honourd them but lou'd the man
because that hee was hee
who since hee has his loue forgone,
& is himselfe noe more,
I loue him not as hee is now,
but as hee was before.

Twixt hope & feare yᵉ best affection sits

Treble : Twixt hope & feare yᵉ best affection sits,
              yᵗ breeds both myrth & Mellancholly fitts

Bass   : what we doe loue we hope shalbe Obtainde,

Treble : yet where we loue we feare to be disdainde;

Bass   : take feare awaye, Affections are but small

Treble : if feare be gone, then there is none at all.

T & B : what most we loue most cause of feare it giues,
              & thus affection in Affliction liues.

B.M.Loan MS.35,f.13.

vnfolde thyne Armes & let me goe

vnfolde thyne Armes & let me goe,
Myne Eyes vpbrayde me of Neglect,
my lips soe close to thyne doe grow,
ye closenes Hynders theyre Aspect!

wee first (saye they) found out her face
and to thy wandringe hart made knowne
the purchase of soe sweet a place
to make a dwellinge of its Owne.

when men A buildinge doe Errect
they giue not drudges soe Much paye
as they doe to ye Archetect
whoe did ye first foundation laye.

Comparde wth vs, what vertue hath
each Other sence since yt it must
alwayes relye vppon Our faythe
And take vp beautye vppon trust

deere Eyes whye doe you soe Complayne
wee dare not Rob you of yor due
for Our Embraces Only Ayme
to humble Eu'rye sence to you.

B.M.Loan MS.35,f.106ᵛ and 122 (without stanza 3).

vnto the soundles vaultes of Hell below

vnto the soundles vaultes of Hell below,
I wayle my greifes remediles Amayne
whylst ffrightfull Ghosts as pittyfull shall show,
& flinty Rockes, remorse take of my paine,
to witnes that my life in noy hath layne
for louers true can neuer dy indeed,
whose loiall Hartes, A Heau'nly fire doth feede.

B.M.Loan MS.35,f.6,f.9.

Virgins as I advise forbeare

Virgins as I advise forbeare,
to followe this bright starre
you might shyne in another spheare,
    but heare Eclypsed are,
for her, your whose sexe I adore,
    and pitty more
those pretious howers you spend
    thus to noe end,
For whoe soe ere you meete or see,
will all her Captiues bee.

But, if uppon this Queene of loue
as Homagers you waite
If as her Guards you neare her moue
    to add vnto her state
Whe[n] she by th'vncontrolled power
    of her Chast flame
Creats a Prince, that hower
    may you the same
And Like to hers, may then your will
haue power to saue or kill.

B.M.Add.MS.31432,f.9ᵛ.

Vulcan Oh Vulcan my deare

Venus	:	Vulcan Oh Vulcan my deare
		give eare & do but heare
		my woefull plight
Vulcan	:	Wt heart of flint can wrong my deare delight.
Venus	:	My wretched boy persues his scorne
		Leaves me wth bitter anguish all forlorne
Vulcan	:	How can he yn do so
		his arrowes have no force weake is his bow
		wast not those pearly dropps in vaine wt power wt might
		can cause this woefull plight.
Venus	:	Alas I yt am Empresse of all hearts
		am beaten thence by his dull leaden dart[s]
		& Cynthia's scornefull female traine
		Hippolitus his rude rout doe number gaine
		& wch is worse ye tamer sort yt shun ye woods
		though Idle cloysterers have no true flame in theire broyld blood
Vulcan	:	O greife O greife
		Lets call some other Diety to send releife
		on Pluto Lett us call
		it is his gold we know yt now does all
		wth yt Ile tipp ye wanton's arrowes yn shall he
		by yt force restore thee to yie Diety.
Ven&Vul	:	Though this be done yet Venus still Complaines
		though she be namd tis Pluto now yt raignes.

Bod.Lib.MS.Don.c.57,ff.12v-13v;43v-44v.

386

Wake oh my Soule awake & raise

Wake oh my Soule awake & raise
up evry part to sing his praise
who from his Spheare of glory fell
to raise thee up from Death & Hell
See how his Soule vext for thy sinnes
weepes bloud wthout feeles Hell wthin
See where he hangs hark how he cryes
oh bitter pangs now now he dyes.

Wake thou much afflicted Man

Wake thou much afflicted Man,
feare not what misfortune can,
Virtue though deprest i' th end
never failes to find a freind,
I thy well wisher com to make
thy mirth increase,
Awake poore soule awake.

Was I to blame to trust thy louelike teares

Was I to blame to trust thy louelike teares,
when 'tis most Just to Judg of others by our owne,
when myne from heades of loue & faith did flowe ;
yet fruitles ran co[u]ld I suspect yᵗ thine
when in my hart each teare did write a line,
should haue no springe but outward showe.

Fitzwilliam MS.52D,f.104ᵛ.

was it A forme, A Gate, a grace

was it A forme, A Gate, a grace,
was it their sweetnes meerly ;
was it the Heau'n of a bright face,
y^t made me loue soe deerlye ;
was it A skin of silke & Snow,
that soule And sences wounded ;
was't any of these or all of these
wheron my fayth was founded ;
Ah noe! 'twas a farr deerer part
then all the rest y^t woñ mee,
'twas A faire Cloathde but faininge hart
I lou'de and has vndone me.

B.M.Loan MS.35,f.57^v.

Wassell wassell wassell wassell

Wassell wassell wassell wassell
thus we frolick frokins all
to ye English Damsell
In a boule like a bell
bring & sing or wassell.

Frokin Francis drink about
here beene Lustick wine & stout
here beene dat will make Love frolick
here beene dat will kill ye Collicke
here beene dat wch never misses
here beene tousand tousand kisses
Here beene ev'ry loveinge thinge
drink good Francis while I sing.

Wassell wassell wassell wassell
thus we frolick frokins all
to ye English Damsell
In a boule like a bell
bring & sing or wassell.

wee doe account y^t Musique good

wee doe account y^t Musique good
y^t issues frō well Tuned woode
y^t better doth ye Eare reioyce
y^t doth proceede frō a sweet voyce
But y^t of all is iudg'd ye Best
y^t comes frō an accordinge Breast

Lambeth Palace MS.1041,f.1.

Wee sing, wee feast, wee Daunce, wee play

Wee sing, wee feast, wee Daunce, wee play,
Garlands wee frame of Flowers & Bay,
in hoñor of yᵉ Jockand May
Welcom all whose ayme's not vissious,
rude, contentious, or malicious,
wee nought but harmless sports intend,
such as would make our Foe our Freind,
They that raile at vs would spare-vs,
yf they knew how well we beare vs.

What art thou what wouldst thou haue?

1   : What art thou what wouldst thou haue?

2   : The shaddow of thy Lover
      that can take no rest in Graue
      till I my greife discover
      in thy Hart I hid a fire,
      the fire of my true paineing
      wch if thou hadst kept Intire
      I had slept without complaining

1   : fright me no more thou wandring ghost,
      turne back thy pale fac'd greeving,
      thy fire went out wth thee not lost
      we liue to loue the liuing

2   : Thy vowes are broake once more take heed
      thy faith shall be rewarded,
      for cuzening me, thy Hart shall bleede,
      thy youth be vnregarded

1   : What shall I doe, *2* : Call back thy vow,
      then sweetly take thy slumbers,
      else endless frights attend thee now,
      and sighing without Number,
      Ile blast thy yoth and on thy Rosy spring
      a dead cold winter, Lame and old Ile fling
      then love to[o] late *1* : O me o me vnfortunate
      though thou be dead Ile love thee euer.

2   : Sleepe sleepe ô sleepe my Ghost shall fright thee never.

1&2   Though fooles secure may kill with theire disdaine,
      Time will at last reward them for their paine
      Harts y^t in Bonde of true love linked be
      nor Time nor Death can sett at liberty.

Bod.Lib.MS.Mus.b.1, ff.74ᵛ-75ᵛ.

What if I dye for love of thee

What if I dye for love of thee,
That very word will murther mee,
Soe shall I purchase lasting fame,
So shall I purchase lasting shame.
>> So shall I liue
>> so shall I dye
>> but I will not trye
>>> nor I
>>> nor I.

What if my loue frō yee I part,
y^t parting sure will break my hart,
fortune Com̃ands it must bee soe,
But love Controwles, yow must not goe
>> I must leave yow
>> then must I dye
>> But I will not trye
>>> Nor I
>>> Nor I.

But tell mee? dost y^u love mee, Deere,
By those bright Eyes of thine, I sweare.
Love then shall all thy freinds destroye
Deere let mee now y^t loue enioye
>> If I deny
>> Then must I dye
>> But I will not trye
>>> Nor I,
>>> Nor I.

B.M.Add.MS.11608,ff.7^v,8.

Wt's a Cuckold learne of me

Wt's a Cuckold learne of me
few can tell his pedigree
or his subtill nature conster
borne a man but dyes a monster
yet great Antiquaries say
they sprang from old Methusaela
who ere Noah's flood was found
had his Crest wth branches crown'd
God in Eden's happy shade
never such a Creature made
yn to cut of[f] all mistaking
Cuckolds are of womens making.

Bod.Lib.MS.Don.c.57, f. 41ᵛ.

What is Freinshipp? but a pleasure

What is Frein[d]shipp? but a pleasure,
             but a treasure,
bred betwixt two worthy spirritts
             by their merritts,
tis two mindes in one meeting,
             never fleeting,
two wills in one consenting,
             each contenting,
one breast in two devided,
             yet not parted
a duble body, and yet single hearted,
two bodyes making one
             throug[h] self Election,
two minds yet haveing both but one affection.

What is Loue besides ye name

What is Loue besides ye name
but a playing wth a flame
or tell w^t is fortune more
y^n a false dissembling whoore
y^t still flatters fooles & Crownes
merritt only wth her frownes
w^t is fame besides a voice
or a hearing of a noyse
w^t is wealth but dust y^ts gay
& quickly flowne away
Loue Fate Fame Wealth all's but disease
y^n w^ts a great man made of these

what man would sojourne heer

what man would sojourne heer,
if Ought we cheifly prize,
a Thousand Hazzards ryse
to make the purchace deere,
and when wth payne and Care tis gott,
we hold it & we hold it not.

B.M.Loan MS.35,f.25.

what shall I doe I'ue lost my hart

what shall I doe I'ue lost my hart,
tis gone I know not whyther;
Cupid cut's strings, then lent him winges,
and Both are Flowne togither!

tell yee ladyes tell, for Loues sweet sake
did any of you finde it
com com it lyes i' yor lips or Eyes
though youle not please to mynde it

pray let me make a search amonge you
in dimples & com to mee
if be not there, o then I sweare
the loss shall ne're vndoe mee

well, is it lost, then farwell Frost
I will enquire noe more
For ladyes they steale harts awaye
but only to restore.

What though my Ms frowne one me

What though my Ms frowne one me
tis but a chance of destiny
& blustering stormes doe but forerunn
ye lustur of a brighter sun
wch when 't apeares Ime full posesest
her frownes weare but in Jest.

Each angry looke appeares to me
but wittness of her modesty
the wiser I haue heard to say
tis darkest before breake of day
why should I curse yt hower of night
that brings A day of light.

I know faire flora in thy brest
a killing anger cannot rest
yet for thy humor I would loue
though thou somtime a fury proue
I know thy soule is so refind
thou wilt At last be kind.

Drexel MS.4041,ff.45ᵛ,46.

when as black night, her vaile displayes

when as black night, her vaile displayes,
And ye Suñ hydes, & steales his light;
wee gazing vp Commend & prayse,
each twinklinge starr of ye Night.

But when ye Sweet Morne 'gins to cleere
and Sol peepes on ye Easterne Maine
all those Faire lights Asham'de t'appeere
before ye Sun, vañish againe

Soe when bright Dian doth Appeere
as beauties Queene Amongst the rest
shee Other beauties Dazz'ls heer
& lights each Soule, & warmes each brest

when Heauen Made her richly faire
Loue joyde, and beinge of a Mynde
shee his lost kingdome Might repaire
Lent her his Eyes, soe became blinde

B.M.Loan MS.35,f.170ᵛ "On the Lady Diana Sidney".

When I Adore you and you haue me in scorne

When I Adore you and you haue me in scorne
faire cruell am I yors or myne by lott
if myne why liue I then of my selfe forlorne,
& liue in you as to my selfe forgott.
why from my selfe to you wth fancye borne
I soe am changde in you that I am not
Only in you depends my lifes sustaine,
nor feare I any death but yor disdayne.

if yrs I am why then soe diffrent are
yr parts of grief that I alone complaine
yet not to plaine alone should be my share,
myne is the greife & yet you feele noe paine
how doe those paines in me procure such care
that you for me in feare of death remayne
yet if my hart be strooke & yrs it be
can you from death & if I dye be free,

Thus loue hath me of his tormenting powrs
Aye me Example made to louers alle
yt yrs I am & yet I am not yors
yors my desyres yr greif doth me befall
& of those bitter sighes my poore hart showrs
ye sound is yors yr torment me doth call
O loue most hard yt if I you Adore
I then am yrs, & if I dye noe more.

B.M.Loan MS.35,f.7.

When I am dead & thou would'st try

When I am dead & thou would'st try
the truth of loues great Mistery
when thou a sparkle dost espy
dauncing before thy brighter Eye,
o doe nott doubt that sparkle Came
from the feruour of my hearte flame
wch thus to prooue open ye vrne,
wherein my restlese Ashes burne,
then rake that dust & thou shalt see
the fire remaine that burnes for thee.

Bod.Lib.MS.Mus.b.1,ff.163ᵛ,164.

When I adore thee

When I adore thee,
sweet & Implore thee
why then vnkindly doost thou frowne on mee
wouldst thou but prou me,
how much I loue thee
o then I know thou soone wouldst pitty mee
Only in you depends my lifes sustaine,
nor feare I Other death then yor disdaine.

doe not dispize me
since thus I prize thee
but cherish wth a smyle my Loue-sick hart
O be thou pleasinge
and giue an Easeinge
to him yt vowes from thee neur to depart
Only in you depends my lifes sustaine,
nor feare I Other death then yor disdaine.

B.M.Loan MS.35,f.182ᵛ

When I was young vnapt for vse of man

When I was young vnapt for vse of man,
I marri'd was vnto a Champion,
Yoᵗhfull and full of vigor, as of bloud,
that vnto Hymens rights full stiffly stood,
but see the luck, this gallant younker dyes,
and in his place an aged father lyes,
weake, pithles, dry, who suffers me all night,
vntouch'd to lye, now full of years & might
When as my former man God rest his spright
girle as I was Tyr'd mee wᵗh sweete delight,
ffor when hee would, then I was coy, and cold
but what I did refuse, now fayne would vse. [I would]
but cannot have, O Hymen yf you can,
give mee those yeares againe, or elce the man.

When sorrowe singes a litle a litles enough

When sorrowe singes a litle a litles enough,
for who will lende their eares to greife?
or what auailes it mee your minde to stuffe,
with longe complaints wch yeldes mee noe reliefe?
I only singe to please my deare
but all in vayne, for shee will neuer heare.

Ø heare my songe o Flora, o heare my songe,
And let relenting teares of mine moue pitty,
Greeuing for my woes which hath binne breeding longe,
Like ioyes abodes breakes now into a ditty :
And I despaire, that makes mee like the swanne
With mournfull notes to singe and dye in one.

Drexel MS.4175.XXvii.

when thou art dead, and thinkst to com

when thou art dead, and thinkst to com
       into Elizium
know I haue barde thy cõminge thither,
wth all my wronges heap'd vp together
     there I haue laide
     before each shade,
the plots where wth thou didst devise
to steale my hart out at myne Eies,
& more to fill thy Tyrranies
thou then those Eye-bals didst draw out
by makeinge me to liue in doubt,
Next, how thou foundst a Subtle way,
to Crucifye me Eu'ry daye
 yet Ne're to take whole life awaye
this my sad storye when they heer,
though blessed soules Nere shed a teare,
yet pitty'inge Me, None will forbeare
their vowes, y^t E-A-Cus would be
as wittye in tormentinge thee.

when thou faire Celia like the settinge suñ

when thou faire Celia like the settinge suñ,
shalt blush to see thy daye is done,
and I A Martyre in thy virgin flame
(thou dead) bespott thy liuinge fame,
and call thee Murderes? then thou shalt see,
thou hast deceaud thy self not me :
when from my Constant Ashes truth shall Rise,
And sylence thy Intended Obsequies :
then, vnpittied thou shalt fall, & wee both dye
by each Others Crueltye
yet pitious fates will not, I dy vnmournd,
Though we both dye, & both dye Scornde.

B.M.Loan MS.35,f.52.

when wee were parted

when wee were parted,
though but for a whyle,
from my brest started
A post Eury Myle;
but I feare, none were derected
from yoᵉ bosome to mee,
for A beautye soe Affected
lookes for loue Custome free.

Tis then noe Merveile
my state should decaye
brought to be servile
And kept from my Paye
but ingratefull to the giuer
know the sea as yoᵉ kinge
can as well Exhaust A Riuer
as you suck vp A springe

And though Triumphinge
you Rowle to the Mayne
small streames are somthinge
And part of yoᵉ traine
vse me gently then that follow
made by Custome soe Tame
I Am Sylent whylst you Swallow
both my teares & my Name.

B.M.Loan MS.35,f.78ᵛ.

Wher shall a man an Object finde

Wher shall a man an Object finde,
that maye preserue a Quiet Mynde;
Sad Sorrow dwels in Loues fayre Eyes,
And beautye Stirrs vp Jellosies;
A Louers hopes, are Mixde wth Feares,
& all his Joyes doe End in teares.

Yet I must Loue, though 't be my Fate
to be rewarded still wth hate;
for by Experience now I feele,
Loue's darts are all magnetick steele
for when I flye to ease my paine,
an Arrow drawes me back againe.

B.M.Loan MS.35,f.172ᵛ.

where shall my Troubled soule at large discharge

where shall my Troubled soule at large
                              discharge,
the Burden of his Siñes; O where,
                              heere,
whence comes this voice I heere
whoe doth this grace Affoord;
if it be thou O lord,
saye if thou heerst my praiers when I call;
                              all;
and wilt thou pittye graunt when I doe Crye;
                              I;
then though I fall, thy grace will my defects Supplye;
                              I;

but whoe will keep my soule from ill,
Quench bad desires, reforme my will;
                              I will:
O may y^t will and voice be blest,
wch yeilds such Comfort vnto One distrest,
More Blesed yet wouldst thou thy Selfe vnmaske;
Or tell at least whoe vndertakes this taske,
                              Aske;
then Quickly speake, Since now wth Cryinge I am Growne soe
    weake;
I shall want force Euer to craue thy Name; O speake
                              O speake
before I wholly wearye Am.
                    I Am.

B.M.Loan MS.35,ff.81,81^v. "An Eccho".

whether away my sweetest deerest

whether away my sweetest deerest
whether away will you depart
will you from mee that should bee neerest
will you from mee yt haue my hart
no no no no bee with mee euer
for on you my ioyes do all relie
say then o say you'l leue mee neuer
for if you forsake mee I must dye

Who sees my face so pale & sad wth greife

Who sees my face so pale & sad wth greife
can hourely tell mee S^r you are in Love
but her faire eye y^t did this anguish move
it sees & knowes yet scornes to give releife

Then will I seeke some beauty y^t is iust
who though she love not shall not Tyronnize
but shall at least confesse y^t in these eyes
there are such passions as her heart may trust

But why speake I of chang as though my will
wch she hath long commanded yet were free
her hate may raigne but not alter me
And therefore let me dying love her still.

Why should y^u be so full of spight

Why should yu be so full of spight
to man, or Woeman kinde?
to say that who are out of sight,
as well are out of minde,
When Cupid showes his equall might,
to people that are blind,

Eyes only may begett that love
that memory must keepe,
and make the sovle to watch and moove,
When they are fast asleepe,
and in sweet Dreames short blessings proove
When wak'ned they doe weepe.

Then be not rash to lay on me,
or any elce this blott,
becavse yt all Mankind by thee
may be soone forgott,
for I must love thee when I see,
and when I see thee not.

Why should yoᵘ thinke me so vnwise

Why should yoᵘ thinke me so vnwise,
or yᵗ I doe discretion lacke
my pretious Jewell to dispise,
becavse hir Haire and eyes are blacke
when as I see yᵗ Heraldry doth yeild
both guiles and argent in a s[a]ble feild

The purer whiteness of a face
shews better when black spots are by
The picture has a lovely grace
whenas the grovnd is contrary
I would leave all thing's else my land, my right
Why not my Mistris then in black and white

The sandy ground is hot but dry
the clay is moist but yet is cold
That shares of each good property
It only is the blackest moúld
Wᶜʰ if yᵉ Tillage and yoʳ corne be right
Will yeild yᵉ richest cropp yᵉ most delight.

Why stayes my floramell where loue

Why stayes my floramell where loue
is but that Apitite
wch doth the sence invite,
Com follow me, & we will proue
what Joyes ye soule delight,

Ascend this flaminge Chariot
wee'le Nimbly Cut ye Ayre,
as doth A virgins pray're,
& as this Orbe below's forgott,
wee'le finde) a place more faire.
      meet)
wee'le finde loues Temple Out where soules
doe mutualy Joyne,
where is nor Myne nor thyne,
where none Obaye wher none Controule,
this is a loue divine.

& whylst our flames together grow
wee'le rayse A Sacred Spire,
wch still shall Mount vp higher
till those yt Gaze on vs below,
shall Call it Heau'nly fire.

B.M.Loan MS.35,ff.59ᵛ,60.

Will you knowe my Mistris face

Will you knowe my Mistris face,
tos a Garden full of Roses,
where the springe in every place,
white and blushing redd discloses,
    tis a Parradice where all
      that attempts ye fruite must fall

Will (you) knowe her forehead faire
tis of Heaven that liveing sp[h]eare
vnder wch the veins like Ayre
all Celestiall blue appeare
    But those burning Sunns hir eyes
    he that dares live vnder dyes.

Will you knowe her body now
tis a tall shipp vnder saile
from Rudder to the prow
nothing but Imperiall
    But that foolish man yt steers
    tells his Compas by his feares.

Shall I now her minde declare
tis the body of a warr
marching in proportions faire
till the lover hopes to[o] farr
    Then her eyes give fyre and all
    within levell helplesse fall.

Will you know

Will you know
    where pleasures grow
& true content abides
    by day it lyes
    fore Shepheards Eyes
at night by Shepheards sides.
ye simple flower is oʳ perfume
ye woolly fleece oʳ rayment
a bower of Eglantine our tombe
not curst for want of payment
wᶜʰ thus much to Princes implyes
He sweetly rests yᵗ sweetly dyes.

Wilt yᵘ bee gon yᵘ hartless man?

Wilt yᵘ bee gon yᵘ hartless man?
heer's none seekes to doe yᵉᵉ Wronge,
heer's food would warme yᵉ Couldest bloud;
Joyes would make an old man younge,
heere are Eyes yᵗ would move
stones to pitty, Rocks to love,
Cheekes of a Vermillion Hew,
sweet as Roses in a dew:
Who but a sylly Swayne or foolish guest,
for homely Cates would leave so daynty a feast?

Wilt yᵘ begon yᵘ frosty man,
is not beauty a faire prize,
do'st rate thy Pelfe wᵗʰ true loves welth
ffoolish man; where are thine Eyes.
Heere are lips both fresh & fyne,
Red as Cherreys in their pryme
Globelike breasts, both smooth & white
full of pleasure & delight,
who but an Ass, would leave such dainty store
to feed on Thistles, when better meat's before.

Goe get yᵉᵉ gone, yᵘ senceless man
& make marts wᵗʰ such as shee
who both in kind & Currish mynd
Ev'ry wayes' as Base as thee.
That hath Eye-lids like some Witch,
wrinckled Cheekes as black as Pitch,
Lypps as pale, & for her Breast,
Lanke, & loathsome as yᵉ rest.
May she disgrace her Sex, & yᵉᵉ so farr
That yᵘ may'st languish t' Death wᵗʰ loathing her.

B.M.Add.MS.11608,ff.20ᵛ,21.

Wth Endles teares, y^t never cease

Wth Endles teares, yt never cease,
I saw a hart lye bleeding,
whose greifes did more & more increase,
her paynes were soe Exceedinge.
When dyeing sighes could not prevaile,
she then would weepe amaine,
when flowing teares began to faile,
shee then would sighe againe.

Her sighes like raging winds did blow,
some greiuous storme foretellinge,
& Tydes of tears did overflowe,
her cheeks ye Rose Excellinge.
Confoundinge thoughts so fyl'd her brest,
shee coold no more contayne,
but Cryes alowd, hath love noe rest,
no Joyes but Endless payne.

B.M.Add.MS.11608,f.15.

With expectation faint & blind; yett still

With expectation faint & blind ; yett still
my soule expects thy promise lord fullfill.
I though a bladder on thy word depend,
confound my foes : when shall my sorowes End ?
The proud haue pitch'ht their Tents, infringd thy lawes :
O sacred Justice snatch me from their Jawes ;
they had almost deuour'd : but I affect,
thy precepts : quicken & by those direct.

Egerton MS.2013,f.52.

wth my loue my life was nesled

wth my loue my life was nesled :
in the somme of happines :
from my loue my life was wresled :
to a world of Heavines :
Ø let loue my life Remoue
Sith I Live not where I Loue

Where the truth once was and is not :
shadowes are but vanities :
shewinge want yet healpe they cannot :
sinnes or slaves of miserie :
painted meate noe hunger feedes :
dyinge life each death exceeds :

Ø true loue since thow hast left mee :
mortall life is teadious :
death it is to live without mee [thee ?] :
death of all most odious :
turne againe and take mee wth thee :
let me dye or live thow in mee :

Ch.Ch.MS.439,f.19.

With silver soundes derived from deepest skill

With silver soundes derived from deepest skill
conduct ye muses to ther sacred hill
pvoke ye sphears wth art drawe downe
the paphian goddes & Latonas sonn
discend yor wayes wth roses & mirths flow
ye same wch in adonis gardins growe.

Roses at first of lillyes hue
till marce adonis did pursue
whome venus rescuinge all in hast
her tender foote a little raste
since Roses have yee tinkture redd
staynd wth the bloud wch bewty shedd.

Woes me alas unblest unhappy I

1.   Woes me alas unblest unhappy I
        ah! me I faint ah! welladay I dy
2.   Speak man of sobs & sighs w^t meane those moanes
        whence flow those teares why those heart-cleaving groanes
1.   Look on a wretch see how I wounded Lye
2.   wth w^t? 1. A shaft ye head's a womans Eye
2.   Their Eyes are soft & could not hurt thee sure
1.   Oh they are hard as Diamonds though pure
2.   Who shot it? 1. Cupid 2. That blind Archer?
        why he cannot see 1. His arrow had an Eye
        Besides his shafts made by his fathers slight
        are tempred soe they cañot fly but right
        Ay me! 2. come weepe no more no more I say
        weel be reveng'd 1. O no hees flowne away
2.   I know old Time y^t is more swift y^n he
        will catch ye boy & bring him back to thee
        And me 1. Will Time doe this 2. He will his bow
        weel break & whip him wth ye string 1. O no
        he'le rage ye more 2. why let him 1. No I see
        a safer way to scape His Tyranny
2.   W^t ist 1. Wee'l take his bolts & head y^m new
        wth woemens hearts & y^n they'le nere fly true.
1&2   Weel take his bolts & head y^m new
        wth woemens hearts & y^n they'l nere fly true

"Mr Rily"

woe is me y^t I from Israell

woe is me y^t I from Israell,
Exjled must in Mesech dwell
& in the Tents of Ismaell.

O how longe, shall I liue wth those,
whose savage myndes sweet peace Opose;
where furye by disswasion Growes.

B.M.Loan MS.35,f.16.

Wooe then the Heauens (gentle loue)

Wooe then the Heauens (gentle loue)
to Melt a Cloud for my releife,
or wooe the deep, or wooe the graue ;
wooe what thou wilt, soe I may haue,
wherwth my debts to paye for greife
has vowde vnless I Quickly paye,
to take both life & loue awaye.

Woods, Rocks, & Mountaynes, & ye desart places

Woods, Rocks, & Mountaynes, & ye desart places,
where nought but bitter Cold & hunger dwells,
heare a poore maids last will kild wth disgraces,
Slyde softly, while I singe yo^u Syluer fountaines,
And let yor hollow waters like sad Bells,
Ringe, Ringe to my woes while Miserable I,
Cursinge my fortunes, drop, drop, drop a teare & Dye.

Greifs, woes, & groanings hopes & all such lyes,
I giue to broaken harts y^t dayly weepe,
to all poore Maids in love, my lost desiringe,
Sleepe sweetly while I sing my bitter Moaninge
And last my hollow lovers y^t nere keepe
Truth in their harts, while Miserable I,
(still) Cursinge my fortunes, drop a teare & dye.

Yee powr's y^t guard loves silken throne

Yee powr's y^t guard loves silken throne
& Judge our passions by your owne,
send downe, oh send y^t golden dart,
wch makes two lovers wear one heart,
Solicite Venus that her doves,
wch through their bills translate their loves,
may teach my tender love and I
to kisse into a sympathy.

Lambeth Palace MS.1041,ff.33ᵛ,34.

You are fayre and louely too

You are fayre and louely too,
all men for yor favors sue,
none can gett it from ye Owner
though they looke loue-sicke vppon her
you doe smyle & laugh at those,
that doe striue to pluck ye rose,
it hath prickles and will scratch them,
y^t presume awaye to snatch them,
be not yo^u too Nigardly,
of those sweets y^t in yo^u lye,
they will fade as yo^u grow oulder,
giue them now therfore ye boulder.

B.M.Loan MS.35,f.28.

You mŭses nŭrses of delights

You mŭses nŭrses of delights
deck ŭp yoŭr temples all with bayes
And celebrat Appollo's rits,
with hymnes and sweet melodioŭs layes.
Come sing, come dance, come sport and play,
for this is great Apollo's day.

The heauens themselves make hermonie
The sea and stars make melodie
birds beasts and fish and every thing
according to their kind do sing
love musick musick musick then
for he yt hates [it] is no man.

you that delight in concord liston all

you that delight in concord liston all
vnto the sacred voyce of harmony
though some doe rise and others fall
it makes them still agree
Even so it is with those
whose mindes heauen doth compose
but were that discord and dissention com
strange kind of musick is wthin y^t rome

Drexel MS.4041,ff.124,124ᵛ.

You that haue been this Euenings light

You that haue been this Euenings light
the honor of this Masquinge night
now sitt you still nor whisper moue
least you offend yᵉ God of Loue
Gods at their banquetts make their choice
to cheer themselues wᵗʰ cleerest voice,
then to euery god assigne
Cups of Nectar heauenly wine
In their boles too let their bee
As in Musick harmony.

B.M.Add.MS.10338, ff. 33-34.

You that haue that daintie eare

You that haue that daintie eare
       & the flintest hart
       Carelesse of loves darte
o that you durst but aproch this voyce to heere
it would humble yor prowde sence
and yor hard harts would mealt yf it once
felt the sweet violl lence
heare the muses in their heavenly quire
wth sweet philomells layes
and mermayds all wth pleasinge tunes conspire
in my devine nimphes voice ther still to prayse
and while the ayre wth her lipes play[s]
it loues to change it selfe ten thousand times [ways?].

Ch.Ch.MS.439,ff.38ᵛ,39.

434

Youre loue if vertuous will shew forth some fruitts of deuotion

Youre loue if vertuous will shew forth some fruitts of deuotion
theres no religion can warrant a dishonest motion
would you entice me to giue you respect
you would not seeke then my honor to Infect
      with poysned potiones
if I euer did affect you twas in honor but in ill ends
I mvst needs neglect you.

That fort is feeble wᶜʰ words can subdue wᵗʰ yᵉʳ battry
tis better stop our eares then leaue vm open to flattery
shall I count yᵗ treu which cannot be Just
youre sighs & sad silence I may not trust
      with eyes so watry
take a louer from a passion like an Image out of date
he stands quite out of fation.

Drexel MS.4041,ff.57-8.

Remember the ende for that makes An end of all thinges

NOTES

LIST OF THE MUSIC MSS. from which the texts have been taken:

	Repository	*Shelf Mark*	
CAMBRIDGE	University Library	MS.dd.3.18.	
	Fitzwilliam Museum	MS.52D.	(John Bull)
	King's College Library	MS.Rowe.2.	(Turpyn's Lute Book)
CONNECTICUT	Yale University Library	MSS.All.a-d.	(Filmer)
EDINBURGH	University Library	MS.Adv.5.2.11.	
		MS.Dc.1.69.	
		MS.490.	(Squyer)
LONDON	British Museum	MS.Add.10337.	
		MS.Add.10338.	
		MS.Add.11608.	
		MS.Add.15117.	
		MS.Add.24665.	(Giles Earle)
		MS.Add.29396.	
		MS.Add.29481.	
		MS.Add.31432.	(William Lawes)
		MS.Loan.35.	(Henry Lawes)
		MS.Egerton.2013.	
	Lambeth Palace	MS.1041.	(Ann Blount)
OXFORD	Bodleian Library	MS.Don.c.57.	
		MS.Mus.b.1.	(John Wilson)
	Christ Church Library	MS.Mus.1022.	
		MS.Mus.87.	(Elizabeth
		MS.Mus.439.	Davenant)
NEW YORK	Public Library	MS.Drexel.4041.	
		MS.Drexel.4175.	
		MS.Drexel.4257.	(John Gamble)
TENBURY WELLS	St. Michael's College	MS.Mus.1018.	
		MS.Mus.1019.	

The MSS will be referred to in the NOTES by shelf mark, only the words Drexel and Egerton being omitted.

List of Abbreviations

Much of the preliminary descriptive and cataloguing work for some of the music MSS. has been done by the present writer in the following series of articles.

Re. MS.Add.31432. "William Lawes' writing for the Theatre and the Court", *The Library,* December 1952, fifth series, VII.4.225-234.

Abbreviation: *WL.*

MS.Don.c.57. "A Bodleian Song-Book", *Music & Letters,* July 1953, XXXIV.3.192-212.

Abbreviation: *ABSB.*

MS.Mus.b.1. "Seventeenth-Century Lyrics, Oxford, Bodleian MS. Mus.b.1.", *Musica Disciplina,* 1956, X.142-209.

Abbreviation: *SCLO.*

Seventeenth Century Songs, (University of Reading School of Art, 1956).

Abbreviation: *SCS.*

MS.Mus.87. "Elizabeth Dauenant Her Booke, 1624", *Review of English Studies,* February 1959, X.37 26-37.

Abbreviation: *ED.*

MSS.1018-1019. "Early Seventeenth-Century Lyrics at St. Michael's College Tenbury Wells", *Music & Letters,* July 1956, XXXVII.3.221-233.

Abbreviation: *ESCL.*

General Note

The following orthographical peculiarities are common to B.M.Add.MS. 29396 and Edinburgh University Library MS.Dc.1.69: the letters "k", "s" and "e" are often undistinguished in form between majuscule and minuscule, both initially and medially. Something of the same difficulty occurs with the letters "w" and "k" in B.M.Add.MS.31432 and with "l" in Bodleian Library MS.Don.c.57.

Textual emendations or suggestions are indicated by square brackets.

NOTES

7 Occurs also in Folger MS.1. 8 (Warwick Castle Ms) c. 1630, f.21 under the title "To his Jealous Mistresse".

10 Extant also in Add.MS.103337,f.47.

11 Extant also in Add.MSS.31432,f.47^v and 11608,f.10^v. *ABSB, WL.* In close proximity to Herrick lyrics.

14 *ED.*

16 Extant also in MS.4257. 34. There are two extra verses from the text printed in *The Thracian Wonder,* 1661.

17 This follows closely on a long group of lyrics by Henry Hughes and is in his style. Cf. Maynard, W., "Henry Hughes: A Forgotten Poet", *Music and Letters,* Oct. 1952, XXXIII.4.345-350.

18 Extant also in Add.MS.24665,ff.55-55^v. Printed by A. H. Bullen in *More Lyrics from the song-books of the Elizabethan age,* (London, 1888), pp. 6-7. Bullen's book is very rare.

21 Extant also in MS.4257. 258.

23 It is difficult to explain the inclusion in a seventeenth-century MS. of this lyric which has most distinct affinities with mediaeval Latin lyrics and compares most favourably with them. Cf. Raby, J., *A History of Christian-Latin Poetry,* (Oxford, 1953). *ABSB.* Line 10: etiam; clari or preferably cari.

25 Extant also in Add.MS.24665,ff.2-2^v.

26 Extant in MS.4257. 21.

28 Extant also in MS.4041,f.139^v.

29 Extant also in MS.4041,f.1 and in MS.Mus.17. *SCLO, ED.*

31 Extant also in MS.4257.186 and Trinity College Dublin MS. F.5.13. 64 ("Gerhard's Mistress' Lament"). Cf. *Roxburghe Ballads,* VI. 563-6—"The Love-sick Maid, or Cordelia's Lamentation for the absence of her Gerhard". Ballad registered 1656. Cf. also Bold, Henry, *Poems Lyrique, Macaronique, Heroique,* 1664, p. 112.

33 Almost certainly by Henry Hughes since it occurs in a group of his.

34 Extant also in MS.2013,f.38^v. *WL.*

36 Cf. *The Musical Companion,* 1667, pp. 198-9. This delightful parody of "Qui laetificat juventutem meam" deserves to be better known.

37 First printed from this MS. by Ault in *A.T.U.L.,* p. 215 and included again here because it belongs to another poem unprinted by Ault which it follows in the MS. The MS. notes that this is an "Answer" to "Farewell all future hope". See p. 103. *ABSB.*

40 This reads to me like Thomas Carew's work.

42 This splendid epitaph on King Charles I was obviously unprinted. See also p. 152.

44 Extant also in MS.4257. 198. Cf. *Select Ayres and Dialogues,* 1652, I.37 and *Wit's Interpreter,* 1655, Sig.V8. It is too good to deserve oblivion. In the 1659 edition of *Select Ayres,* p. 45 there is a possible attribution of the poem to Thomas Jordan.

46 Extant also in Edinburgh University Library Adv.MS.5.2.14,f.5^v and in Add.MS.24665,ff.80-80^v. Cf. John Forbe's, *Songs and*

Fancies, 1662, 53; Terry, C. S., "John Forbe's 'Songs and Fancies'", *Musical Quarterly*, October 1936, XXII.4. 402-419 and Diem, N, *Beiträge zur Geschicte der Schottischen Musik im XVII Jahrhundert*, (Zürich, 1919), pp. 75-6 where the 5.2.14 text is given. The text is given here because Diem's book is so rare and inaccessible.

47 This is almost certainly by Thomas Carew since it occurs in a strong group of his lyrics. Cf. *Wit's Interpreter*, 1655, Sig. Q8.

50 Extant also in MS.87,f.6v. A play song? *ED*.

53 This is attributed to Winchilsea in *Ayres and Dialogues*, 1653, I.17.

55 Extant also in MS.52D,ff.101ᵛ-4 and ff.105ᵛ-7. *ESCL*.

60 Extant also in MS.1041,ff.17-8. It occurs here in MS.Loan 35 in a group of Henry Hughes' poems.

61 Extant also in MS.4041,ff.73ᵛ-5. *SCS, SCLO*.

63 Some of the lyric has not been filled in in the MS.

64 Extant also in MS.4041,ff.126-6ᵛ and in Add.MSS.29396,f.21 and 11608,f. 73, the latter containing the note that another chorus was added to it "31 Oct. 1659".

67 This sounds to me like Alexander Brome's work.

69 This occurs also in Folger MS.1.8.f.27ᵛ. *WL*.

70 Surely this is a Masque song. Printed by A. H. Bullen, *More Lyrics* . . . , (London, 1888), p. 20.

71 Line 13. Xant: Xanthus. Ovid. *Her.v.*29-31; *Met.II.*245.

76 One of the "Songs made for some Comedyes 1631 Sʳ R. Hatton", according to the MS. note.

77 Extant also in MS.2013,f.44ᵛ.

78 Extant also in MS.4041,f.16ᵛ. *WL*.

83 The MS. note illustrates one of the peculiar problems of seventeenth-century music MSS:— "This & yᵉ other page 71" (i.e. "Though yᵒ determine not to Loue"—p. 365 here) "I had of my Cos; H: Hyde at the same time" (i.e. 13 Oct. 1660) "I put yᵉ Base for him in yᵉ 3. songes". Only *two* songs in the MS. as it now stands are marked as having been sent by Hyde.

84 Extant also in MS.4257. 183. *WL*.

90 Extant also in MS.4175, xlvi.

97 Extant also in Bodleian Library MS.Mus.Sch. F.575,f.6ᵛ. *ED*.

99 Extant also in Add.MSS.29481,f.13ᵛ and 24665,f.12ᵛ. It is mentioned by title only in the Table to MS.4175, xxxii. It is included also in Folger MS.2073-4,f.28ᵛ. The MS. note here says "My lady Killegrewe". Cf. Neilson, G., "A Bundle of Ballads", *Essays and Studies*, 1921, VII.108-142 where the first and last lines are given and the poem is attributed to Francis Beaumont. Cf. also Jamieson, R., *Popular Ballads*, 1806, II.299-300 where it is described as coming from a "MS.Collection in the possession of my late excellent and much regretted friend, MR. BOUCHER of Epsom".

100 The first stanza was printed in Alfonso Ferrabosco's *Ayres*, 1609, v; the second stanza given here would seem to be unknown.

101 I owe the correction "lead apes" from my printing in *ESCL* to Thurston Dart, Fellow of Jesus College, Cambridge.

102 Extant also in Add.MS.29396,ff.30ᵛ-1.

104 Extant also in MS.4257. 187. Cf. *Loyal Garland,* 1686.

107 Extant also in Add.MS.29396,f.57 and in Ch. Ch. MS.438,f.1 (Mrs. Anne Baylie her Booke 1645).
MS.29396 has an ascription of this and a second part "Laugh not fond foole"—p. 211 here—to "Sʳ Tho: Nott". *SCS,SCLO.*

108 Extant also in MS.4257. 171. Cf. *Wit's Interpreter,* 1655, Sig.V7. *WL.*

112 Extant also in MS.4257. 113.

114 Dowland's *Second Booke of Songs,* 1600, ii, but a different order and a better one than that printed by Fellowes. This is the famous pavan "Lachrimae" extant also in Add.MSS.24665,ff.7-7ᵛ, 33933,f.86 and in MS.1018,f.30ᵛ. I include it here because Ch.Ch.MS.439 preserves a much better order of the lines than that printed by Fellowes, E. H., *English Madrigal Verse,* (Oxford, 1920), p. 421, the usually received text. *ESCL.*

115 Another of the "Songs made for some Comedyes 1631 Sʳ R. Hatton".

116 Extant also in MS.4257. 93.

117 Cf. *Wit's Interpreter,* 1655, Sig.Z8ᵛ. *ABSB.*

120 *ED.*

125 This occurs also in Folger MS.2071-7 (Joseph Hall's Commonplace Book) with the title "written by Thomas Earle of Straford 1641".

130 Extant also in MS.4257. 13, MS.1041,ff.2ᵛ-3, Add.MS.34800,f.33 and in MS.4175 xvi only the last four stanzas occurring in the last named MS. Printed by Jamieson, R., *op. cit.,* II,307-8 "From a Collection of Songs and Sonnets in MS. in the British Museum, Bibl.Harl.212.7.Plut $\frac{8}{vi}$ c".

132 MS. leaf ends before bracketed material. Annotators have suggested the ending.

134 Extant also in MS.4257. 30.

135-36 Pausanes is the name of a character in Thomas Killegrew's *The Prisoners,* 1640, Sig. B2.

137 This comes at the end of a long list of Thomas Carew's lyrics in the MS.

141 Extant also in MS.4041,ff.110ᵛ-1ᵛ and in MS.Loan 35,f.162.

146 Can this be Robert Herrick's? It follows immediately on three Herrick poems.

147 Extant also in MS.Mus.b.1.,ff.120ᵛ-1. *SCS, SCLO.*

151 Extant also in MS.Loan 35,ff.32ᵛ-3.

155 Extant also in Bod.Lib.MS.Mus.Sch.F.575,f.5ᵛ. *ABSB.*

156 Extant also in Add.MS.24665,ff.36-36ᵛ. A play song? The refrain of "Domingo" links it with "Samingo". Cf. the present writer's article, "Some incidental music newly discovered for *2 Henry IV",* *Shakespeare Quarterly,* Autumn 1956, VII.4. 385-393 and Sternfeld, F., "Lasso's Music for Shakespeare's 'Samingo'", *Shakespeare Quarterly,* Spring 1958, IX.2.105-116.

158 Extant also in Add.MS.11608,f.57ᵛ, MS.4257. 270 and MS.490. 68. Cf. *Select Ayres and Dialogues,* 1652, I.21.

159 Extant also in MS.2013,f.14.

Page

162 Obviously this is a companion poem to Sir Henry Wotton's "How happy is he borne or taught". *ABSB*.

163 Extant also in MS.Don.c.57,f.97ᵛ. *ABSB*.

164 Another of the "Songs made for some Comedyes 1631 Sʳ R. Hatton".

165 The MS. contains an additional stanza to the printed version in Alfonso Ferrabosco's *Ayres*, 1609, x.

167 Extant also in MS.4257. 162. The second stanza is written out in the MS. in 5 long lines ending with the rhymes "striues", "wiues", "frowne", "downe" and "muche". I have broken up the lines into more regular lengths.

169 This is the "First part" to "Now I haue found"—p. 246 here. *SCS,SCLO*.

175 Extant also in Add.MS.29396,ff.79ᵛ-80 and in MS.4041,ff.18ᵛ-9. *SCLO*.

176 Extant also in MS.4257. 306.

177 Extant also in MS.4257. 199. Cf. *Select Ayres and Dialogues*, 1659, p. 22.

178 Campion's lyric is extant also in Add.MS.15117,f.19. The MS. here preserves extra verses to the version in John Dowland's *Third Book of Aires*, 1603, xvii, and to Thomas Campion's *Fourth Book of Ayres*, c.1617, xvii.

180 Extant also in Add.MS.103337,f.50 and MS.Loan 35,f.29ᵛ. *ABSB*.

186 Extant also in MS.439,f.22ᵛ. Both MSS versions contain an extra stanza to the received version in Thomas Bateson's *Second Set of Madrigales*, 1618, iv.

189 Extant also in MS.4257. 228.

191 Extant also in Add.MS.11608,f.55ᵛ and MS.4257. 216.

198-99 Extant also in Add.MS.29396,ff.113-113ᵛ, 11608,ff.23ᵛ-5ᵛ. The MS. has the title "The Witch of Endor". Cf. Martin, L. C., "A Forgotten Poet of the Seventeenth Century", *Essays and Studies*, 1925, XI. 5-31. One of Nathaniel Wanley's poems is called "The Witch of Endor" but is a long rambling piece and much less effective than the present text.

204 This would seem to me to have formed part of a Masque entertainment.

211-12 See *supra* p. 107. *SCS, SCLO*.

213-14 The following annotation occurs in the MS:—"A pastorall. Cantors: Hirrus yᵉ father pyrrhon yᵉ sonne Ornone A mornefull Sheperdes for the Loss of Laron". The Latin names would seem to be made-up ones.

215 Extant also in MS.4257. 261. Cf. *Select Ayres and Dialogues*, 1652, I.36 and *Wit's Interpreter*, 1655, Sig.V3.

217 Extant also in MS.2013,f.25ᵛ and MS.Loan 35,f.87ᵛ. It occurs in Folger MS.1.8,f.26 ascribed to "Mʳ Reynolds". *ABSB*.

220 MS. annotation—"ffebr 16 1641. To my honourd ffriend Sidney Berd esqʳ".

224 Bracketed line supplied by an annotator.

226 Extant also in Add.MS.29481,f.23. Cf. Thomas Morley's *First Booke*, 1600, ij and iij, Sig.A3; both versions would seem to have a common source.

Page

227 Extant also in Add.MS.15117,f.6.

230 Extant also in MS.4257. 28.

233 See *infra* p. 435.

236-37 Extant also in Edin.Univ.Lib.MS.5.2.14,ff.1-1ᵛ. Cf. Diem, N., *op. cit.*, pp. 67-8 where the full text from Adv.MS.5.2.14 is given.

242 Extant also in MS.4257. 188. Cf. *Select Ayres and Dialogues,* 1659, p. 65.

243 Can this be Edmund Waller's? It is immediately followed by a close group of his.

244 Extant also in MS.4041,f.59ᵛ.

246 Cf. *supra,* p. 169.

250 Cf. Bantock and Anderton, eds., *The Melvill Book of Roundels,* (Roxburghe Club, 1916), pp. 43-4 and *Deuteromelia,* 1609, vii Sigs. C2ᵛ-3. Is this a burlesque of John Mundy's "Of all the birds that I have heard" in his *Songs And Psalmes,* 1594, x?

251 Cf. *Select Ayres,* 1669, p. 63.

252 Extant also in MS.4041,ff.1ᵛ-2. *SCLO.*

253 Extant also in Add.MS.29396,ff.84ᵛ-5 and MS.2013,f.32.

255 Extant also in MS.2013,f.24 and in Ch.Ch.MS.434,f.2.

256 This is almost certainly by Henry Hughes occurring as it does in a strong group of his.

257 Extant also in MS.Loan 35,ff.136-7.

258 *ED.*

263 MS. ends before bracketed material.

270 Extant also in Add.MS.31432,f.29ᵛ. *WL.*

271 This is almost certainly by Thomas Carew; it occurs in a long group of his poems. Extant also in MS.4257. 241.

277 Surely this belongs to a dramatic context?

289 Extant also in MS.Loan 35,f.47ᵛ.

294 Extant also in Edin.Univ.Lib. Adv.MS.5.2.15. Printed in *England's Helicon,* 1600 and ascribed to "I.G."

296 This splendid parody of "Per saecula saeculorum" shows the continuity of the *Carmina Burana* spirit. Cf. Schmeller, J. A., *Carmina Burana,* (Breslau, 1904), p. 236 no. 175, "In taberna quando sumus". Lines 2, 3, 4 supplied by annotator.

298 Extant also in MS.Don.c.57,f.50, Add.MS.11608,f.32ᵛ,MS.2013,f.37ᵛ and MS.4257. 214. *ABSB.*

303 William Strode's poem is extant also in MS.Dc.1.69.167 and MS. 1041,f.3. Two more verses occur here in MS.Don.c.57, hence my reason for including it. *ABSB.*

304 Extant also in MS.2013,f.35. *ABSB.*

308 Extant also in MS.Mus.87,f.16ᵛ. The dramatic context suggests one similar to the mourning over Imogen in *Cymbeline.*

311 Robert Herrick? *SCLO, SCS.*

314 This occurs in Folger MS.1.8,ff.9-9ᵛ attributed to "Mʳ Raynolds".

316-17 Extant also in MS.4257. 100. *SCLO, SCS.*

319 This, I feel, may well be Thomas Carew's occurring as it does in a strong Carew group.

Page

321 Extant also in MS.4257. 112. A dramatic context?

324 Extant also in MS.4257. 27.

329 This occurs in a strong Thomas Carew group.

330 Extant also in MS.2013,f.43. *SCLO.*

331 This occurs in Folger MSS.1.8.f.30 and 2073-3,f.2 ascribed to "Zouch:Townely". *SCLO.*

336-37 Extant also in Add.MS.31432,f.22ᵛ. *WL.*

338 Professor L. C. Martin, the latest editor of Herrick (1956), agrees with me (by private letter) that this *may* be Herrick's. *SCLO, SCS.*

341-42 Extant also in Add.MS.29396,ff.87-9 and from the line "Come away 'tis night" to the end in Ch.Ch.MS.438,ff.1ᵛ2. *SCLO, SCS.*

344-45 MS. interlineation, stanza 4, lines 3-4:—*Seale*
The printed leafe to print againe
Or light a flame wᵗ hand will proue.

351 Cf. John Forbe's, *Songs and Fancies,* 1662, 43. *ABSB.*

352 Printed by A. H. Bullen in *More Lyrics from the song-books of the Elizabethan age,* (London, 1888), p. 111. Only 250 copies of Bullen's book were printed.

355 Extant also in Add.MSS.17786-91,f.8ᵛ and in MS.Rowe 2. 6.

360-61 Extant also in MS.4257. 264.

362 This belongs to a line of conjurations and is possibly dramatic in origin. *SCLO.*

363 Extant also in MS.4257. 226 and MS.Loan 35,f.33.

365 Cf. *supra,* p. 83.

368 Mentioned by title only in MS.4175, xviii. The MS. version here contains an additional stanza to the received version in Walter Porter's *Madrigales and Ayres,* 1632, xi.

369 Cf. *Wit's Interpreter,* 1655, Sig.Z6.

370 Cf. *Select Ayres,* 1659.

376 *ED.*

378 Extant also in MS.Loan 35,f.14. *ABSB.*

381 Extant also in MS.4041. 26 and in Add.MS.29396,f.48ᵛ.

384 This occurs in a strong group of lyrics by Thomas Carew. Extant also in MS.4041,f.33ᵛ, and MS.4257. 225.

395 Extant also in Add.MS.29396,ff.53-53ᵛ.

397 This is included in the Folger Commonplace Book MS.2073-3.91 and is extant also in MS.Dc.1.69. 182.

401 Extant also in MS.4257. 180.

404 Cf. *Ayres and Dialogues,* 1669, p. 50. *SCLO, SCS.*

406 Included in the Folger Commonplace Book, MS.2073-3,ff.31ᵛ-2. *SCLO, SCS.* Line 11 and bracket material line 12 from Folger MS.2073-4.ff.31ᵛ-2.

408 This occurs in a Herrick group. Æacus, line 17, a judge in Hades.

413 *ED.*

415 Extant also in Add.MS.29396,ff.92ᵛ-3 and in MS.4257. 253. *SCLO.*

417 Extant also in MS.2013,f.36.

418 Extant also in MS.Loan 35,f.50 and MS.Dc.1.69. 119.

419 Extant also in MS.Mus.b.1.,f.20. *ABSB, SCLO.*

421 Extant also in MS.4257. 232.

423   Cf. Thomas Morley's *First Booke,* 1600, iiij and John Forbe's, *Songs and Fancies,* 1662, 45.

428   Extant also in MS.Don.c.57,f.6 and MS.Mus.87,f.11. *ED.*

431   Extant also in MS.Don.c.57,f.51 and Add.MS.24665,ff.58-58^v. *ABSB.*

433   One of the "Songs made for some Comedyes 1631 Sr R. Hatton".

435   The second verse only occurs in MS.Dc.1.69.157. "My loues as vertuous" (p. 233 in this present collection) is described in MS.4041 as "ye answer" to this poem. See *supra,* p. 233.

SUBJECT INDEX

PROPER NAME INDEX

FIRST LINE INDEX

451